GUIDE TO FURNITURE STYLES:
ENGLISH AND FRENCH

Guide to
Furniture Styles:
English and French

1450 TO 1850

JOHN GLOAG

F.S.A., HON.F.R.I.B.A., HON.F.S.I.A.

ILLUSTRATED BY

MAUREEN STAFFORD

A.R.C.A.

ADAM & CHARLES BLACK
LONDON

FIRST PUBLISHED 1972: A. & C. BLACK LTD., 4, 5 & 6 SOHO SQUARE,
LONDON W.I

THIS BOOK IS COPYRIGHT UNDER THE BERNE CONVENTION. NO
PORTION MAY BE REPRODUCED BY ANY PROCESS WITHOUT WRITTEN
PERMISSION. ENQUIRIES SHOULD BE ADDRESSED TO THE AUTHOR'S
LITERARY AGENTS: A. D. PETERS & CO, IO BUCKINGHAM STREET,
ADELPHI, LONDON, WC2N 6BU, OR GEORGES BORCHARDT INC.,
145, EAST 52ND STREET, NEW YORK, N.Y., 10022, U.S.A.

© 1972 JOHN GLOAG and MAUREEN STAFFORD
ISBN 0 7136 1267 3

PRINTED IN GREAT BRITAIN BY
W & J MACKAY LTD, CHATHAM

CONTENTS

DEDICATED TO ALICE WINCHESTER

The idea of this book arose from your suggestion that I should write about English furniture in the French taste for *Antiques*, so very properly this study of the relationship between French and English furniture design is dedicated to you, and the dedication also marks many years of friendship.

JOHN GLOAG

ACKNOWLEDGEMENTS

Many of Maureen Stafford's drawings have been made from examples in the Victoria and Albert Museum and the Wallace Collection, and I am grateful to the Directors for permission to reproduce them. I must also acknowledge the help I have received from the Prints and Drawings Department of the Victoria and Albert Museum and from the Print Room of the British Museum. Line drawings have been used throughout supplemented by engravings reproduced from contemporary sources or from the works of John Henry Parker and Thomas Wright, to which acknowledgement is made in the captions. In Sections 11, 12, 14, and 16, I have incorporated some paragraphs from articles published in the magazine *Antiques*.

J.G.

ORIGINS OF STYLE IN FURNITURE

Mediaeval craftsmen in France and England were not conscious of working in any particular style as we now understand that term; they impressed regional characteristics on many of the things they built and made, establishing and developing what we now call the Gothic tradition, though the word *Gothic* was not introduced until the 17th century, when it was first used to distinguish mediaeval from classic architecture. The term style, long associated with literature, was not used to describe specific types of architecture until the 18th century, nor was it generally applied to the design of furniture and the character of furnishing until the 19th, when it replaced the word taste. Both terms were used by King in the "Address" to *The Modern Style of Cabinet Work* (second edition, 1832), when he wrote: "As far as possible, the English style is carefully blended with Parisian taste . . ."

Between the 13th and 15th centuries furniture was simple in construction; the skill of carvers supplied such forms of ornament as roundels in geometric patterns, like those on the front of the boarded chest on the next page. Such devices were unrelated to prevailing architectural ornament; but by the late 14th century the decoration of furniture, and sometimes the shape, reflected contemporary architectural design; a relationship that survived throughout the four hundred years between 1450 and 1850, the period covered by this book. Until the opening of the 16th century, a family likeness existed between French and English furniture, for in both countries carpenters, joiners, carvers and painters followed the virile Gothic tradition: in England, the last phase of Gothic, Perpendicular, was comparable with but more restrained than the French, Flamboyant.

During the second half of the 15th century, boarded construction was superseded by joined construction. The former had been practised by carpenters, who used split or sawn planks for receptacles and seats, putting them together and holding them in place with iron nails, pegging them at the angles with oak pins, and reinforcing the ends of chests with cross-pieces. Joined construction depended on the use of the mortice-and-tenon joint, usually secured by pegs or dowels without glue, so that stability was gained from structure, not from weight. This improved the form of chests, plate

A 13th-century boarded chest, decorated with three roundels of chip carving. Carvers invented and executed such forms which, at that date, were seldom influenced by prevailing architectural ornament. *In the Victoria and Albert Museum.*

cupboards, and seats; cupboards and beds became freestanding, released from dependence on a wall; chairs were lighter, and more mobile; and the relative simplicity of furnishing at that time is shown opposite, by two illustrations drawn from contemporary manuscripts. Trestle tables appear in both drawings; a joined seat in the upper, a settle in the lower, and fireplaces flanked by columns in both. The central hearth in lofty halls, like that at Penshurst Place on page 12, continued in use during the 16th century, but for some two hundred years solars and parlours had budded off from the large, communal living spaces; such small, intimately furnished rooms revealing an increasing desire for privacy that reflected social changes.

Life for the wealthy in the late Middle Ages was animated by fashions that affected clothes, ceremonial armour, weapons, the design of jewellery and plate, and the pattern and colour of fabrics. Noblemen and prosperous merchants enjoyed the trappings of luxury without the consolation of comfort. The interiors of great houses in France and England glowed with tapestries, silks and velvets. Panelled or plastered walls and coffered ceilings were brightly painted; the preponderance of richly decorative fabrics is shown by the 15th century hall on page 10, and the brilliancy and variety of the colours are described in the detail of the state chair on page 11. Cushions and the voluminous clothes worn by men and women, modified the asperity

8

Above: Hooded fireplace, flanked by columns; board-ended stool, with pointed arches pierced in uprights; and trestle table.

Below: Low-backed settle with rudimentary linen-fold device and ball finial; and a trestle table. Both drawn from a 15th century manuscript in the Bodleian Library. Ref. Canon, Liturg, 99. Reproduced from Parker's *Domestic Architecture in England*, Oxford, 1859.

of hard, flat, wooden seats; but joiners made no concessions to human contours, and upholsterers were concerned only with curtains and bedding.

Consciousness of style developed with the Renaissance more rapidly in France than in England, where the revival of Roman architecture and classic ornament was resisted by masons, carvers and woodworkers, who copied

9

Interior of a 15th century hall, showing the conspicuous part played by decorative fabrics in late mediaeval furnishing. A high-backed chair of state stands on the dais, with a curved canopy above, suspended from the ceiling; a plate cupboard, covered with fabric, projects at right angles from the wall, with a platform behind it for the butler. The guests are seated on low-backed settles, watching the antics of a jester. This simplified drawing is copied from a brilliantly coloured interior depicted in a M.S. of Quintas Curtius in the Bodleian Library. (Ref: 751 127R.A.) Reproduced from Parker's *Domestic Architecture in England*, XV Century, Part I. (See opposite page.)

Detail of the chair of state and the flanking seats, with the figures omitted. The surmount of the chair, rising to a finial, is carved with contemporary Gothic ornament. In the original coloured illustration, the surmount and the frame of the chair are gilded, the back panel is vermilion, and the plate cupboard covered with a bright crimson fabric. The fabric on the steps, the dais, and the flanking seats, is sky blue, the same material being used for steps and seats.

what they called "Italianate" motifs, but were unable to interpret them, or to understand the system of design the orders of architecture represented. French craftsmen, receptive and original, were less conservative and far more enterprising; they mastered the classic idiom, which gave France a long start in the development of distinctive styles in furniture and interior decoration. The old mediaeval family likeness between the furniture of the two countries disappeared in the 16th century; though until the end of the 17th, English design lacked the vivacious and often capricious inventiveness that gave France the artistic leadership of Europe. The similarities and differences between French and English furniture styles are described in sections that follow.

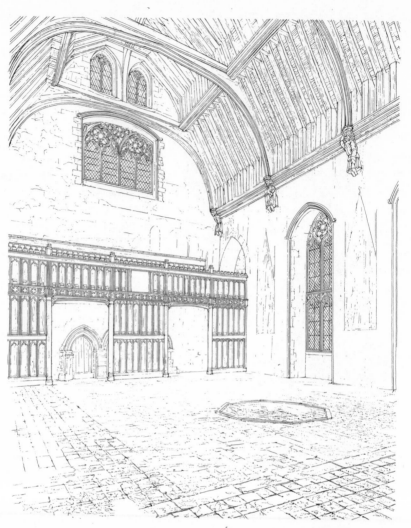

Above: The Great Hall, Penshurst Place, Kent: mid-14th century. The screens date from the late 16th century, and include some modern work.
Right: The central fireplace in the Great Hall. The double-ended fire dog, mediaeval in design, dates from the 16th century. Reproduced on a smaller scale from a drawing by F. W. Fairholt, included in *A History of Domestic Manners and Sentiments in England,* by Thomas Wright. (London: 1862.)

SECTION I. THE GOTHIC TRADITION. 1450–1550.

The study of style is inseparable from the study of design, and during the 15th century the character of furniture design was gradually changed, partly by structural innovations that improved the shape and convenience of receptacles, tables and seats, and partly by the introduction of better heating methods and technical advances in the manufacture of glass and the manner of glazing. Wall fireplaces and weather-proof windows revolutionised the furnishing of rooms, large or small. In France, many great mediaeval castles were transformed into luxurious chateaux; in England, as the need for fortification receded, spacious, airy country houses were built, freed from the limitations imposed by thick walls and narrow window openings. The well-lit hall of Ockwells Manor, illustrated on the next page, is different in scale and conception from the Great Hall at Penshurst Place, shown opposite. Just over one hundred and twenty years separate those two interiors; but they clearly belong to different patterns of social life.

Amenities indoors were amplified after the central hearth was supplanted by fireplaces with flues rising to external chimney stacks, such as those shown on pages 14, 15 and 16. Wall fireplaces had been built as early as the 11th and 12th centuries, and by the late 15th were becoming a dominant feature in the decoration and arrangement of rooms. Those depicted in contemporary drawings were often hooded, like the examples on page 9, top right of page 15, and the top of page 17; and in the bedroom interior on page 16, the rudiments of a chimneypiece are suggested by the recesses above the fireplace opening. In England at that period the fireplace did not project from the wall; the opening was usually headed by a Gothic arch, surmounted by arcading and castellated ornament, as at Southwell Palace on page 15, or flanked by attached columns supporting a narrow shelf, with characteristic Gothic mouldings and spandrils, those elongated triangular spaces formed above the line of the arch. Spandrils were sometimes filled by carved ornament, but in the hall fireplace at Ockwells, page 14, they are undecorated. Such simple types of brick or stone fireplace persisted until the mid-16th century, their proportions related to the surrounding wall panelling, as in Wolsey's Closet at Hampton Court on page 34. The projecting chimney

Part of the interior of the Hall, Ockwells Manor, Bray, Berkshire. This half-timbered house, built *circa* 1465, had by the mid-19th century become partly ruinous, and an illustration in Parker's *Domestic Architecture in England,* shows the exterior overgrown with creepers, and with many of the windows blocked up. (Oxford: 1859. Vol. III, Part II, plate facing page 278.) Release from the needs of fortification and improvements in glass-making led to the expansion of windows, which ascended through two storeys as bays, and ran above the panelled walls, forming a transparent frieze. *Right:* Fireplace in the Hall at Ockwells.

Left: Fireplace at Southwell Palace, Nottinghamshire, with Gothic arcading above the arch, surmounted by castellated ornament. The arch of the fireplace is flush with the wall. 15th century.

Right: Fireplace with hood: French, 15th century. (Compare with illustrations on pages 9, 17, and 30.) Drawn from a MS. in the Bodleian Library. Ref. Canon, Liturg. 99. Included in Parker's *Domestic Architecture in England*. (Oxford: 1859.)

breast that ascended to the cornice was a later development, which eventually became a massive feature of carved wood or stone or moulded plaster, with figures, columns or pilasters flanking the fireplace opening and supporting an entablature and ornamental or heraldic panels above, or a repetition usually on a slightly smaller scale, of the figures or columns, thus forming a single, imposing decorative unit.

The chimneypiece increased the dominance already established by the fireplace, and altered the focal point of social life. Directly the source of heat was transferred to one wall of a room, seating arrangements and seat furniture were radically changed. In mediaeval halls people sat on benches and chests drawn up against a wall, with a hanging called a dorcer or dorcel suspended at the back to protect those seated from chilly contact with stone or plaster. A large dorcer is shown on the wall below the musicians' gallery in the interior on page 10, hanging behind the low-backed settle that accommodates three people. In the original illuminated MS, the dorcer is coloured vermilion and patterned with gold arabesques, and a bright green cloth, called a banker, drapes the seat and footboard of the settle. Such strips of cloth were also used on the top of chests, though not on the example before the fire in the bedroom on page 16. Chests continued to serve as seats in France through-

Bedroom interior, 15th century, drawn by F. W. Fairholt, from a MS. of Lydgate's Metrical Life of St. Edmund (MS. Harl. No. 2278). This shows a more elaborate type of chimneypiece, with recesses above the fireplace opening, and firedogs supporting the logs.

out the 16th century, and in English country houses for at least one hundred years later.

Our knowledge of seat furniture in the mid-15th century is derived largely from contemporary drawings; chairs, stools and settles had long existed, and seats of straw and wickerwork had been in use for hundreds of years, but actual examples of more solidly constructed seats are rare. Little has survived, apart from fragments like the right hand section of the triple throne from the Great Hall of St. Mary's Guild, Coventry, on page 20, though a few pieces of English and French household furniture made in the last years of the century have been preserved. That fragment from Coventry shows how woodworkers interpreted Gothic tracery and ornament that masons had originated in stone. The use of blind tracery on wood surfaces by carvers and

16

Late 14th or early 15th-century French bedroom interior, drawn with the figures omitted, from a miniature in *Histoire de la Belle Hélaine*. (*National Library, Paris.*)

Bedroom interior, French, late 14th century, showing settle, small table, and high-backed armchair. The bed, supported on a wooden frame, has a half-tester. Drawn, with the figures omitted, from a miniature in *Othea*, a poem by Christine de Pisan.

Late 15th century French plate cupboard, with canopy and pierced tracery in cupboard doors. From a drawing by Henry Shaw, but with the plate omitted. Shaw's original drawing, taken from a MS in what was then the King's Library, Paris, was included on plate XXV of *Specimens of Ancient Furniture* (1836).

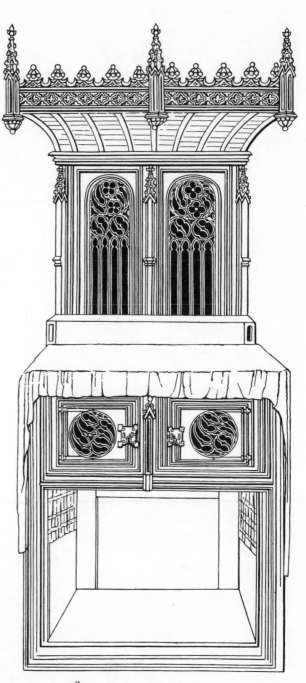

18

joiners was far more than the transposition of ornament from one material to another. Those craftsmen, working with a more tractable material than stone, gave a new, crisp definition to Gothic forms, and although the debt to an architectural prototype is apparent in the French plate cupboard opposite, a far more fluid and independent use of tracery and ornament appears on the chest at the top of page 22 (a so-called "Flanders" chest, that may have been made by Flemish craftsmen working in England), and the French oak chest and walnut dresser on pages 23 and 25. Craftsmen in both countries had a common approach to the use of Gothic ornament; the treatment of the vertical columns that divide the panels on the two chests is similar, and the way tracery is handled is far more lively and flexible than the geometric rigidity of the simple pattern on the English desk on page 21.

English and French carvers began to associate decorative devices of their own invention with traditional Gothic ornament, and of these the linenfold panel is the best known. This was introduced, probably by Flemish craftsmen, during the latter part of the 15th century, and may originally have been a

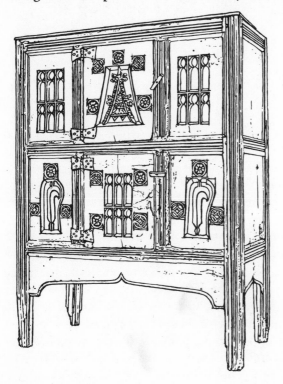

Food cupboard, with pierced panels for ventilation. English, *circa* 1500. After the second quarter of the 16th century the name "Livery cupboard" was used for this type of receptacle. *In the Victoria and Albert Museum.*

19

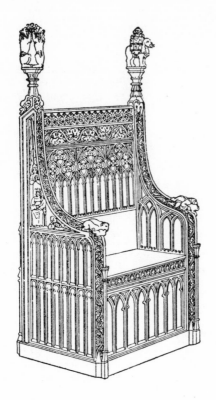

Mid-15th century oak chair, with blind tracery and carved Gothic ornament. This was formerly the right–hand seat of a triple throne on the dais of the Great Hall, St. Mary's Guild, Coventry, made for the Masters of the united guilds of St. Mary, St. John the Baptist, and St. Catherine. The finials are sur-mounted by the royal lions of Eng-land, and the arms of Coventry. *After Richard Bridgens.*

symbol for use on the panels of chests and cupboards where napery, bed linen, or scrolls of parchment were kept. Before the end of the century it was used on wall panelling as well as furniture in France and England; while regional variations appeared in Northern and Central Europe. The panels of the high backed chair in the bedroom at the bottom of page 17, and on the side of the settle on page 30 (top left), anticipate the linenfold device in an elementary, simplified form. How greatly the device could be varied is illustrated by the early 16th century English chest on page 26, the sideboard in the centre of page 27, and the panels at the sides and below the seat of the French chair at the right of page 31. Another decorative device, that had no prototype in architectural ornament, was used on panels in the late 15th and early 16th centuries, and consisted of two curved ribs, formed by two ogees set back to back, with vine leaves and tendrils, bunches of grapes, and fleur-de-lys carved in the spaces between the ribs and sides of the panel. This has been called a parchment or parchemin panel, and an early 16th century example is shown on page 26. Heraldic emblems, and naturalistic motifs occasionally adorned the panels of framed and joined chests, like the standard chest on page 22, and the headboards of beds, like the example on page 36.

During the second half of the 15th century the variety of furniture was greatly increased. The cupboard, that had originated as a recess in the thickness of a wall, enclosed by wooden doors, became a free-standing piece of furniture, often used for storing food, with pierced panels provided for ventilation, like the English type on page 19, originally called an aumbry and, by the second quarter of the 16th century, a livery cupboard. ("Liveries" were small quantities of food and drink provided for guests when they went to bed; a mediaeval custom that survived in England until the 17th century.) The plate cupboard, for storing and displaying gold, silver and pewter, also developed. The forerunner of such display cupboards is shown at the right of the interior on page 10, with vessels set out on the stepped stages, and a platform at the back for the butler; and from this, more elaborate types evolved, like the tall French example on page 18, that has a central storage

Oak desk, with hinged lid. English, *circa* 1500. Blind tracery and arcading decorate the back and sides, and the plain front is ornamented by two carved lion masks at the upper corners. A view of the back is shown to the right. *In the Victoria and Albert Museum.*

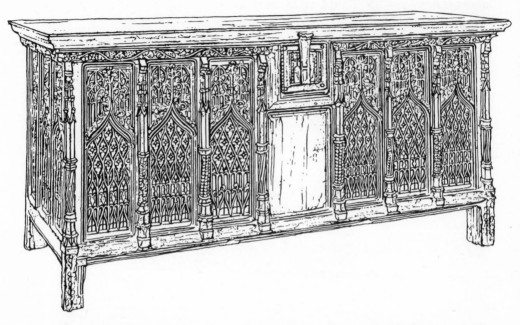

Late 15th-century chest, with elaborate tracery. A so-called "Flanders Chest", probably made by English joiners and ornamented by Flemish carvers. Intricate Gothic tracery, borrowed from architectural prototypes, was used by English, French and Flemish craftsmen. Compare this example with the French chest opposite.

Framed and joined standard chest, English, late 15th century. Heraldic devices and formalised flowers and foliage are carved on the panels. From Rockingham Castle, Northamptonshire. *After Parker.*

Carved oak Gothic chest, French, late 15th century. Like the example opposite, contemporary architecture has inspired the carver's work. See also illustration on page 25. *In the Victoria and Albert Museum.*

unit with pierced roundels in the doors, a superstructure known as a desk forming a background of Gothic tracery for cups, vessels and dishes, surmounted by a canopy, and a solid base below, providing additional display space. The French dresser, on page 25, was closer to the sideboard in purpose, and the two English sideboards, late 15th or early 16th century in date, on page 27, are serving tables, with cupboards below. (The spurious term "credence table", that dates from the 19th century, is sometimes wrongly used to describe such articles.) The mediaeval word *board* was applied according to some specific function: such as cup board, dressing board (from which dresser is derived), meat board, moulding board, oyster board, and so forth. The term board was also used for a table, which in mediaeval houses did actually consist of a board or slab of wood, supported by trestles, like those illustrated on page 9, or on a frame if it was permanent or fixed, when it was known as a table dormant or dormante. (The supports of tables were still called dormants or dormans as late as the 17th century in England.) Boards with trestles could be quickly dismantled, to free space in a hall or dining

23

parlour, but by the early 16th century, extending or draw tables were made, with three leaves, those at each end sliding out from below the centre leaf, which dropped down into the vacant space, so that a long, level surface was available. An English draw table in oak on page 27, has four legs, linked by stretchers below, and a shaped supporting frame under the top. The need to save space exerted a growing influence on the structure and design of tables and cupboards, when rooms were more intimately furnished. During the first half of the 16th century furniture, especially seat furniture, lost much of its former solidity, which also saved space.

The settle usually had a hinged seat, with a receptacle below, and occasionally entered into partnership with a wall, like the angle settle on page 30. A broad bay window, such as that at Thame Park on page 35, was often fitted with a seat. Chairs, benches and stools became lighter, easier to move about, and the stiff immobility of the high-backed, ponderous state chair, like the French examples in the bedroom at the bottom of page 17 and those on page 31, or the solid oak joined English chair on page 33 (at the left), were replaced by more graceful and far more comfortable types, such as the triangular-seated turned chair and the coffer-makers' chair at the top of page 32. In France a light form of conversation chair was invented, with a flat, semicircular seat, an upright, slightly tapering back, and elbows supported by uprights; this "Caquetoire" type came to England in the second quarter of the 16th century, and the back of the example on page 33 is carved with Renaissance ornament, which also appears on the upper back panel of the heavy oak chair beside it. (A later and far more sophisticated design appears on page 46.)

Gothic and Renaissance ornament was at first uneasily associated on French and English furniture; in both countries craftsmen were reluctant to abandon established methods, and in France, during the first half of the 16th century, they seemed to be conducting a resistance movement, for the Gothic tradition, persistent and powerful, influenced domestic architecture in the style of Francis I, which exhibited evidence of conflict between designers and masons. That conflict was soon resolved, but in England it became apparent later, and continued until the early 17th century. French furniture makers carved and applied classic motifs with a mediaeval ruggedness; while the work of English carvers remained tentative and uncertain for nearly a hundred years.

Decorative fabrics continued to play an important part in furnishing, not only in such incidental and supplementary articles as cushions and bed hangings, but in the surface substance of some types of seat furniture, such as

Late 15th century walnut dresser, carved with tracery, less elaborate than the example on page 23, but also exhibiting a close relationship to the last, Flamboyant period, of French Gothic architecture. Linenfold panels appear at the back of the open base. *In the Wallace Collection.*

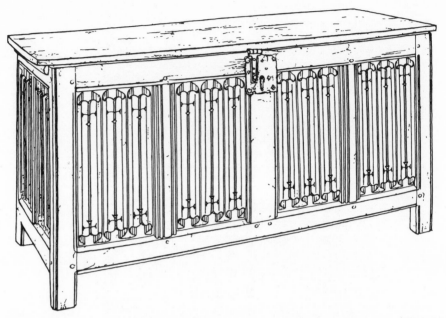

Early 16th century joined chest, carved on the front and side panels with the linen-fold device. Examples of linenfold panels appear on the side of the low-backed settle, page 9; the lower part of the French dresser, page 25; the sideboard opposite; the interiors on pages 34 and 35; and the chair, page 33. *Reproduced by permission of the late R. W. Symonds.*

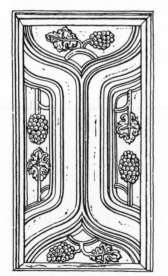

Parchment or parchemin panel, *circa* 1530. Sometimes described as a rib panel. Like the linenfold pattern, this was invented and used by carvers, and was not derived from architectural ornament.

Late 15th or early 16th-century English sideboard, with heraldic devices and tracery carved on the front panels.

Sideboard with linenfold panels. English, late 15th or early 16th century. This type of sideboard has often been wrongly described as a credence.

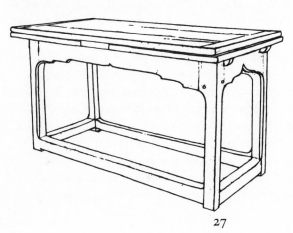

English draw-table in oak, first half of the 16th century: the native Gothic tradition persisted throughout that century, and far into the 17th, and appears in the furniture made by country craftsmen. *All three examples in the Victoria and Albert Museum.*

coffer-makers' chairs. These were chairs with leather-covered frames, produced by a cofferer or coffer-maker, a specialist craftsman, primarily a leather worker, who covered coffers and travelling chests with leather. The frames of such chairs were X-shaped, and the example on page 32, top right, was originally covered in velvet. The slung, cushioned seat was far more comfortable than the flat, wooden seats of joined or turned chairs and benches. Folding chairs with X-shaped frames were in use in Italy and France during the 15th century; they frequently appear in contemporary manuscripts, and this type of frame when used on a non-folding chair supplied a broad seat, and the austerity of leather as a frame covering gradually gave place to velvet and embroidered fabrics. In England the coffer-makers' chair was developed and improved in comfort throughout the 16th century. The loose cushions used on flat wooden seats were stuffed with down, feathers, or hair, enclosed in cases of leather or woven fabric. In England the craftsmen who stuffed cushions and beds and cut and sewed bed curtains belonged to the Upholders' Guild, that was established during the second half of the 15th century, and the name upholder survived until the Victorian period, when it was replaced by upholsterer, though both terms had been used concurrently in the late 18th and early 19th century.

Mediaeval beds were structurally dependent on one or two walls of a room, with curtains that could be drawn across the open sides to enclose the bed completely, and a canopy suspended from the ceiling beams. When free-standing beds came into use in the 15th century, curtains and canopy were separated from the wooden bedstead, like those illustrated on pages 16 and 17. The post or posted bed, with a canopy or tester supported by two columns at the foot and a tall headboard called a selour or sellore, was independent of walls or ceiling, and when the curtains were drawn it became a room within a room. The example on page 36 that dates from 1530 is the ancestral type of the beds later known as four post or four posters, a contemporary term applied to all varieties of canopied beds when the tester completely covered the bed area, whether it was supported by four posts or two posts and a headboard: the term half-tester denoted a canopy projecting from the headboard and covering only part of the bed, like that at the bottom of page 17. The exposed wooden headboard was usually panelled and decorated with carving, like the bed on page 36, which is in the native English style, slightly influenced by the Renaissance. Very few beds of this early date have survived in France; but contemporary illustrations suggest that until the mid-16th century fabrics generally concealed the wooden framework, though the bed

Oak form, with shaped ends. Compare the arched openings at the ends with those of the stool at the top of page 9. English: late 15th to mid-16th century. *Victoria and Albert Museum.*

Above: Oak bench with shaped and pierced underframing, and a bar linking the buttressed ends. Late 15th to mid-16th century: Welsh. *In the collection of the National Museum of Wales.*
Left: Board-ended stool in oak. English, early 16th century. The shaped ends and the arched openings in them, reproduce on a smaller scale those on the oak form at the top of the page.

29

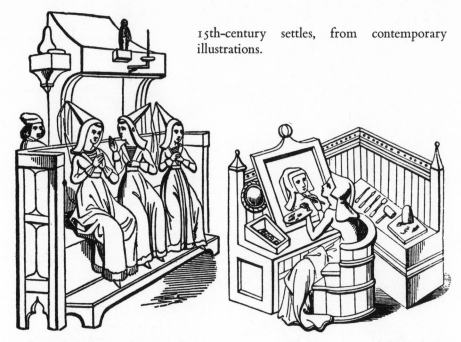

15th-century settles, from contemporary illustrations.

Left: High-backed settle with foot-rest. From an illuminated MS. by Froissart. (British Museum. MS. Reg. E.2.)
Right: Angle settle and chair with concave back. From the illuminated MS. *Boccace des Nobles Femmes*. Both drawn by F. W. Fairholt, and reproduced from Thomas Wright's *A History of Domestic Manners and Sentiments in England* (London: 1862).

High-backed, long settle, with upright members terminating in ball finials. Drawn from a 15th-century manuscript in the Bodleian Library. (Ref: MS. Bodley, 283, fol. 59R.) Reproduced on a slightly smaller scale from Parker's *Domestic Architecture in England*, XV Century, Part I, following page 114. Compare with low-backed settles on pages 9 and 10, and the angle settle above.

15th century French
state chairs.

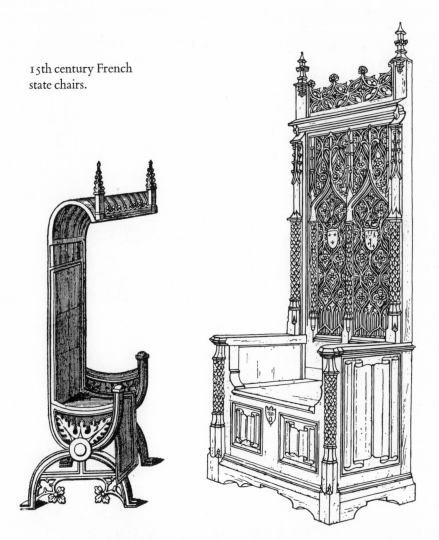

Left: High-backed chair with canopy, drawn from the French MS. "Roman de
Renaud de Montauban", and reproduced from Shaw's *Specimens of Ancient Furniture*. *Right*: Chair with Gothic tracery carved on the back panels, and Gothic cresting and finials. Linenfold panels are carved on the sides and below the seat rail.

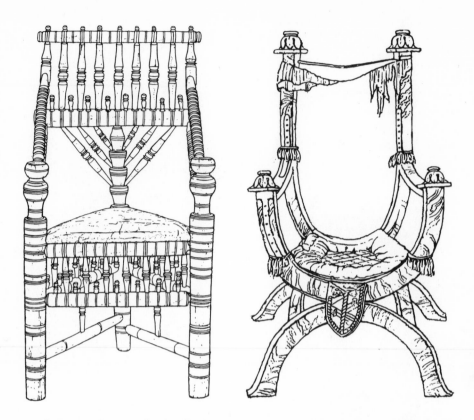

Left: Triangular-seated turned chair, with ornamental spindles, and front legs prolonged to form arm supports, the third leg rising above seat level to support the back. English: first half of 16th century. A comparable example is in the Ashmolean Museum, Oxford. By the end of the century turned chairs became elaborately decorative. (See page 63.) *Right*: Coffer-maker's chair; the X-shaped frame originally covered in velvet; after an example in the Vestry of York Minster. Late 15th or early 16th century.

at the top of page 17 has a headboard with two linenfold panels, and a plain footboard. Descriptions of luxurious furnishing suggest that tester, headboard and counterpane were often of matching material, and when the envoy of the Duke of Burgundy was entertained by Edward IV in 1472, the bed in the luxurious apartments prepared for him had a "Counterpoynte clothe of golde, furred w^t armyn" [ermine] and "the Tester and Celer [selour] also shyninge clothe of golde. . . ."

By the beginning of the 16th century the ideas of fashionable architects began to affect the character of French furniture; in England the native Gothic style survived, unchanged by the preliminary experiments with Renaissance architecture and ornament, made by a few wealthy men, like Wolsey, who employed Italian artists; and even such limited Italian influence was soon replaced by French, for during the second quarter of the century France was the source of inspiration for Renaissance design. Although the family likeness between the furniture of the two countries was lost, a new relationship was

Left: Oak joined chair, with the linenfold motif on four of the panels, and the upper panel of the back carved with Renaissance ornament. *Right*: Oak armchair, *circa* 1535, with carved back and shaped apron below the seat. This Caquetoire type, derived from France, was developed throughout the 16th century, and a later example is shown on page 46. Both English examples indicate that the Gothic tradition, though still determining form and sturdy construction, was now competing with "Italianate" fashions in ornament. *In the Victoria and Albert Museum.*

33

Fireplace and linenfold panelling in Wolsey's closet, Hampton Court. Early 16th century: *circa* 1525. No concessions to Renaissance ornament disturb the placid comfort of the native English style. The proportions of the fireplace are related to the panelling.

formed, and French and English taste was thereafter affiliated, with periodic fluctuations of intensity, until the mid-19th century. Periods of taste tend to merge into each other. A style that makes a complete break with tradition has an emphatic identity, a disruptive character usually indicative of social, cultural and economic changes. In England the native style generated in the mid-15th century was disrupted a hundred years later as a result of cultural changes reinforced by a social and economic revolution. In France cultural changes alone were sufficient to acclimatise the Renaissance.

Bay window at Thame Park, Oxfordshire. Early 16th century. The walls are covered by linenfold panelling from floor to frieze, with Renaissance ornament above, interpreted by craftsmen working in the Gothic tradition, who imparted more vigour than delicacy to the wreaths, medallions and classic acanthus foliations. Bay windows of this size could accommodate a table and chairs for such informal meals as breakfast: frequently, long seats were fitted, the back formed by the panelling.

English posted bed, with ornament carved in the
native style, as yet barely affected by Renaissance
fashions. The front posts and the selour, the tall
headboard, support the tester; separate posts support the front of the bedstead. A detail of one of
the lower panels of the headboard is shown to the
right. *Drawn from the original example in the Victoria
and Albert Museum.*

SECTION 2. THE RENAISSANCE IN FRANCE

The naming of specific styles of furniture is a comparatively modern habit: in the 18th century various fashions were described in terms of *taste*, perhaps as a tribute to their ephemeral nature; but when makers and their patrons spoke of furniture in "the Gothick" or "the Chinese" or "the French" taste, they were not consciously classifying a style; they were using a modish label for what was often little more than a transitory vogue. Furniture historians have since used a variety of descriptions for periods of design, generally taken from the name of a dynasty or a monarch, beginning in the 16th century with Tudor or early Tudor, though that native English style had only acquired a recognisable national character when Henry VII began his reign in 1485. No comprehensive and relatively simple names may be given to comparable French work, for what is generally and rather loosely described as the First Renaissance or Francis I style includes the reigns of Charles VIII, Louis XII, and Francis I, a period extending from 1483 to 1547. The early Tudor and Francis I styles were concurrent in time but divergent in character, for the Gothic tradition, perpetuated in England, lost the battle for survival in France, where furniture craftsmen came increasingly under the control of architects, and although they might resist the imposition of the classic idiom they had to please their patrons, which they did with progressive servility for the next two hundred years, suppressing imaginative gifts that were henceforth exercised only by joiners and carvers who served the needs of small landholders, farmers and thrifty peasants.

The early interpretations of Renaissance ornament came from the hands of carvers who decorated the panels and frames of the strong, sturdy chests, dressers and seat furniture made by joiners who were still working in the Gothic tradition. The chest on page 38 and the dresser on page 39, carved in low relief with acanthus foliations, scrolls, medallions and figures, are far more accomplished in execution than the panels on the backs of the two English chairs on page 33, though all these examples lack the spontaneity and boldness of traditional carving. The former freedom of expression enjoyed by carvers and woodworkers was already undermined by two influences, one commercial, the other professional.

The chest above and the dresser on the opposite page illustrate the confidence of French carvers when interpreting Renaissance ornament. Both examples date from the second quarter of the 16th century. The horizontal mouldings on the lid and base of the joined chest unite the panels of carved ornament.

Printers in Flanders and Germany had, early in the 16th century, discovered the commercial possibilities of copy books; they employed illustrators and engravers to fill plates with versions of the classic orders of architecture, and inventive draughtsmen created such new forms of ornament as strapwork, with scrolls and arabesques, enclosing diamond and lozenge-shaped patches, shields and cartouches, intermingled with scraps of classic detail. The plates of such books imposed two-dimensional conceptions of ornament on men hitherto accustomed to work in the round, men who knew how to manipulate shadows with mouldings and carved enrichment. Consequently much of the early 16th century Renaissance decoration was deprived of the high lights and shadows that had given such a rich texture to Gothic carving. This addiction to low-relief was a passing phase, though the influence of the copy books remained, and by the close of the century French carvers were giving distinctly unorthodox renderings of classic ornament, associated with strapwork, executed with buoyant vitality, like the carved walnut dresser on page 42. The carved oak bedstead on page 45 exhibits a comparable association of classic detail and strapwork.

The professional influence was exerted by architects, whose activities were gradually segregated from those of masons, joiners, carvers and other execu-

French dresser, *circa* 1540. The massive treatment of the supports and the moulded detail of the base, show the persistence of an old tradition: Renaissance ornament has been used to decorate a Gothic frame.

Above: Chimneypiece with Renaissance ornament, from Maison Lebours à Cusset.
By the mid-16th century French designers were regulating their work by the rules
and proportions of the classic orders, although they took discreet liberties with
decorative details, as exemplified by the pilasters flanking the fireplace opening, with
their dwarf Ionic capitals and paw bases. The figures and foliations in the panel
above the mantel and the herms on either side of it, retain a suggestion of Gothic
vigour without the bold ruggedness.

Right: Chimneypiece in the style of Francis I, from Hotel Lasbordes à Toulouse.
First half of the 16th century. Classic proportions provide the framework for the
closely-packed ornament, preserving clarity of detail, and avoiding the appearance
of overcrowding. Although the Italian origin of the ornament is obvious, the French
national genius for handling ornamental composition is asserted.

See caption on opposite page.

41

Dresser of carved walnut, *circa* 1600, a form comparable with the English court cupboard of the late 16th and early 17th century. The boldness and vitality of the carving owes something to the persistence of the Gothic tradition, though the character of the ornament, especially on the panel at the back of the lower, open tier, and the gallery that surmounts the upper part, recalls the plates of the Flemish and German copy books of architectural detail that were produced throughout the 16th century. Compare the ornamental treatment with that of the cupboard opposite. *In the Wallace Collection.*

tant craftsmen; their exclusive preoccupation with the refinements of the classic orders and composition on a grand scale, to please the nobility and gentry for whom they worked, generated class consciousness in art; furniture design and interior decoration ultimately became complementary activities, subservient to fashion, originating on the architect's drawing board and not on the craftsman's bench. As a master of classic idiom, who recognised the orders as a universally applicable system of design, the architect assumed control of many crafts. The chimneypieces on pages 40 and 41 are examples of that control; they have a sophistication of design that only a subtle and sympathetic knowledge of classic proportions and detail could achieve; com-

Late 16th century cupboard of carved walnut in two stages. This is an architectural design; proportions and details are of classical origin, and the carved figures are drawn from pagan mythology. Hecate is represented by the applied caryatid figure in the centre of the upper part, between the cupboard doors, which each bear the figure of Abundance, standing in arched niches flanked by satyrs. The drawer fronts are carved with trophies of arms, the doors of the cupboards below with grotesque masks and chimeras, and the stiles occupied by three herms. The composition shows a closer and more sympathetic knowledge of classic ornament than the dresser on the opposite page. *In the Wallace Collection.*

pletely different in character and conception from the examples of what may be called carvers' classic on pages 42 and 43. On those chimneypieces nothing has been left to the carver save his skill.

The quality of social life was changing. The design of seat furniture suggested that manners were easier and more informal; chairs lost their mediaeval identity with the stateliness of high rank. Princes, noblemen and great ecclesiastics still had their chairs of state, highbacked, canopied and magnificent with carved ornament; but smaller and less ponderous seats were introduced, lighter in construction and easy to move, like the conversation chairs on pages 33 and 46. Towards the end of the 16th century the back stool appeared, first in France and later in England. As the name implies, this was a stool with a back which increased the comfort of the dining parlour where seating arrangements were now radically different from those of the great hall in a mediaeval house. Nobody in the mediaeval household was allowed to forget the importance of rank and station; the master of the household, his wife, and perhaps an important guest were alone favoured with chairs, and they sat at a high table on a dais at the end of the hall, overlooking two or three other tables set at right angles at which the poor relations and the lower orders were seated on benches or stools. Conversation at the high table was limited, because the host and his guests could only speak with comfort to those on their immediate right or left; to address anybody else they had to lean forward and raise their voices. At the lower tables, where people faced each other, conversation was easier, though it was probably subdued out of deference to the exalted occupants of the dais; certainly in France where respect for rank was more firmly established than in England. The stiffness and restraint imposed by the nature of a communal hall were diminished by the privacy of the dining parlour where the host sat on a chair at one end of a long table, with the hostess on a chair at the other end; the guests had benches or stools until their comfort was increased by the back stool, which, because it was armless, was not dignified by the name of chair. (The term back-stool was still used in England as late as the third quarter of the 18th century.)

Extending tables were improved in design; but the simplest type of table, the long board covered with a cloth, supported on trestles and easily dismantled (like those illustrated on page 9), remained in use from the 15th to the late 17th century, even in the well furnished houses of prosperous merchants and tradesmen, where one large, overcrowded apartment frequently combined the functions of kitchen, dining room and bedroom. (See page 71.)

44

Carved oak bedstead, massive in structure, with a Gothic arch and Renaissance ornament. The date 1562 is carved on the lower member of the cornice. This medley of unrelated motifs exhibits the incertitude of contemporary craftsmen; loyalty to tradition is apparent in the execution of carved detail, which, while acknowledging prevailing fashions for classic motifs, is still Gothic in feeling. The influence of popular copy books of architectural detail is disclosed by the strapwork panels at the head. Design is still in a phase of transition. Litchfield, who gives the provenance of this example, states that it was originally in the Chateau of Pau.

Above, left: Broad-seated, joined arm-chair, with arcaded back, elaborately carved cresting, and the arch motif repeated below the seat. *Above, right:* Back stool with turned legs and open back.

Right: Conversation chair: a later and more refined development of the English type shown at the bottom right, on page 33. The carved panel in the back is framed by a simplified version of guilloche ornament.

All three French examples date from the second half of the 16th century.

46

Carved table, with fluted columns separated by arches, supporting the ends, and three turned members rising from the stretcher. The turned uprights, like those on the bed on page 45, are independent expressions of the turner's craft, unrelated to contemporary Renaissance fashions. Late 16th century.

Tables with elaborate underframing acquired an architectural character, like the table *à l'italienne* above, with fluted columns separated by arches supporting the ends, richly carved decoration, and three turned members rising from the stretcher. The broad-seated armchair on page 46 has three front legs in the form of columns; an arcaded, slightly inclined back, with identical arches repeated below the seat; the top is surmounted by florid scrolls, flanking a mask. The back stool on the same page has legs turned to imitate Tuscan columns, and pendant scroll-work below the top rail of the open back.

The structural form of beds changed very little after they became free standing at the end of the 15th century, and in France and England the posted type introduced a lively decorative interest in addition to the richly embroidered fabrics that had, hitherto, concealed the wooden framework. The columns supporting a tester with frieze and cornice, the frame that held the bedding, and the high headboard, were all carved with versions of classic ornament. Occasionally the columns were replaced by herms, caryatides or atlantes; sometimes such figures were repeated on the headboard, though more often that feature was carved with grotesques and strapwork ornament, derived from the plates of Flemish copybooks. The massive oak bedstead on page 45 illustrates the incertitude of mid-16th century carvers, whose loyalty to tradition was in conflict with their obligation to acknowledge prevailing fashions of ornament. Such elaborate structures were exceptional, and by the second half of the century, French carvers were using the copy books of ornament with greater discretion and interpreting classic detail with informed judgement. Very few beds survive from this period, though contemporary illustrations suggest the persistence of the late 15th century types, with heavy curtains and valances hiding the structure.

Among other contributions to furnishing, French makers introduced the day bed, the ancestor of the 18th century duchesse, and various forms of sofas designed for reclining. Furniture makers in France had by the close of the 16th century, become the humble and obedient servants of fashion, directed by the trained imagination of some singularly brilliant architects, who were also the humble and obedient servants of their aristocratic patrons, whose taste for the visual refinements of life transformed furnishing into a fine art.

SECTION 3. ELIZABETHAN AND JACOBEAN

When Elizabeth I began her reign in 1558, furniture was still Gothic in character; staid and solid in construction, enlivened by an occasional flourish of Italianate ornament, but closely identified in general design with the native English style that had matured early in the century. It was very different from the flamboyant, richly carved furniture which later expressed the taste of the bustling, buoyant, adventurous age that we think of as Elizabethan; an age of emphatic individuality and growing wealth, when men of property desired visible evidence of their prosperity, as they did some two and a half centuries later in the Victorian period. During the fifty years between 1575 and 1625 this new, rich, copiously decorative furniture style was perfected by carvers of commanding ability who interpreted the classic orders of architecture with blithe irreverence for the correct proportions of columns and capitals, mingling antique ornament with strapwork and devices of their own invention. Periods cannot be measured by fixed years; in every century English and French styles had forerunners and survivors; Jacobean design was a continuation of Elizabethan; the two periods flowed into each other, and late 16th and early 17th century furniture is almost indistinguishable.

The illustrations of this section show a progressive understanding of the significance of the classic orders as a system of design, partly owing to the influence of the theatre, because the settings devised by Inigo Jones for the masques and plays that entertained the Court of James I enlarged the artistic education of royal and noble patrons, increased their appreciation of the subtleties of "Italianate" architecture, and later amplified that appreciation by buildings of incomparable grace, like the Banqueting House, Whitehall (1619–22). Late Elizabethan furniture and interior decoration was uninfluenced by this architectural enlightenment, though carvers and joiners seemed to be dimly aware that classic architecture had something more to offer than a convenient treasury of ornament. For example, the posted bed on page 51, dated 1593, exhibits dexterity in composition, especially in the ornamental treatment of the head; and although outrageous liberties are taken with the posts, the Ionic capitals that crown them are correct in form and detail, so

49

are the moulded and panelled plinths below, while the proportions of the tester follow the horizontal divisions of a classic entablature. The bulbs that break the lower part of the posts have the characteristic gadrooning that Mr Edward H. Pinto has aptly named "cup and cover", for the domed top of the bulb resembles a cover for the lower, cup-shaped part. This was a favourite device, used also on the melon-shaped bulbs of table legs, the posts between the tiers of court cupboards and the recessed upper part of press and hall cupboards. Sometimes gadrooning was confined to the "cover", with crisply carved acanthus foliations adorning the "cup", as illustrated by the court cupboard on the lower part of page 54, the press cupboard on page 55, and the draw table in the Bromley-by-Bow room on page 56.

Turners also contributed to the decoration of furniture and woodwork; split balusters and spindles were applied to flat surfaces, like those on the stiles of the chest on the lower part of page 52, the pilasters of the chimneypiece on page 59, and the uprights of the arched back stool on page 64. The round-headed arch, frequently used as an ornamental device, both in France and England, appeared on bed heads, chimneypieces, chair backs, cupboard doors and the fronts of chests. Variations of the arch form on three chests are shown on pages 52 and 53, and arcading was occasionally used as a frieze in a panel-led interior. On page 52 the upper example, inlaid with architectural perspectives in bogwood and holly, is a type imported from Germany, and possibly made by German or Flemish craftsmen working in England. As the buildings depicted on the front bear a superficial resemblance to features of the Palace of Nonsuch, that Henry VIII began to build in 1538 at Cheam in Surrey, they have become known as Nonsuch chests. The twin arcaded panels on the front, flanked by pilasters from which the arches spring, are topped by pediments, boldly outlined by chequered inlay. On page 53 two lavishly decorated English chests are illustrated, both with arcaded panels and herms carved on the muntins and stiles. The ornament on the upper example betrays the unsettling influence of the Flemish and German books on archi-tectural ornament, which often confused English carvers, who by attempting faithfully to reproduce motifs engraved on the plates inhibited their own vigorous invention and debilitated their powers of composition. The other example on that page boldly adapts classical motifs: compare the carving of the herms on both chests: those above are crude, primitive and static; those below have an explosive vitality, fantastic and grotesque like all the fanciful semi-human figures and fabulous hybrids that were recaptured from classical antiquity by Renaissance artists and architects. This particular chest is dated

Continued on page 58

English posted bed in walnut, dated 1593. The fluted posts are tapered above, surmounted by Ionic capitals, broken by bulbs below, decorated with gadrooning, and
rising from plinths that stand free of the bed frame. The frieze of the tester is inlaid
with an heraldic emblem, a corbeau, the crest of the Corbets. The two arcaded panels
at the head are separated and flanked by dwarf pilasters, tapering towards the base,
with Ionic capitals, and carved consoles above. Classic ornament has been used
with discrimination to enrich the mouldings on the head and tester. The bed,
originally at Astley Corbet in Shropshire, is now in the *Victoria and Albert Museum.*

51

Above: Oak chest, late 16th century, with architectural perspectives inlaid in holly and bogwood. Chests of this type were made in Germany, frequently imported, and also made by German craftsmen in England. As the architectural subjects have a superficial resemblance to Nonsuch Palace that Henry VIII began to build at Cheam in Surrey in 1538, they are known as Nonsuch chests. Fred Roe suggested that the inlaid designs may have been inspired by Nonsuch House, a timber building, pre-fabricated in Holland, sent to England in sections, and erected on London Bridge in 1577. The arcaded panels on the front are flanked by pilasters and crowned by pediments. *In the Victoria and Albert Museum.*

Below: Joined chest in oak, probably of west country or Welsh origin. *Circa* 1620–30. The muntins between the panels are carved with grotesques, and the scrolls on the top rail alone suggest the influence of classic ornament. Split balusters are applied to the stiles.

Above: Chest with arcaded panels, late 16th or early 17th century, with herms carved on the muntins and stiles, and rudimentary Ionic capitals above them. Gadrooning enriches the mouldings above and below the arcaded front, and the ornamental details suggest the influence of Flemish and German copy books. *Reproduced by courtesy of the late R. W. Symonds.*

Below: Oak chest inlaid with marquetry; arcaded panels appear on the front and at each end; the herms carved on the muntins and stiles are far more vigorously executed and bolder than those on the upper example. The base is fitted with three drawers. *Circa 1595. Reproduced by courtesy of the Trustees of the Lady Lever Art Gallery.*

Left: Court cupboard, early 17th century, with strapwork carved on the upper and lower tiers, and columns with Ionic capitals between the tiers. *In the Victoria and Albert Museum.*

Right: Court cupboard in walnut and oak, with carved bulbs on the front supports of the tiers, Ionic capitals above, and inlaid ornament below the gadrooning of the upper tier. *Circa* 1600. *Reproduced by courtesy of the Trustees of the Lady Lever Art Gallery.*

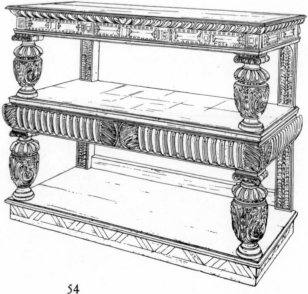

English press cupboard in oak, dated 1610. The carved pilasters, with Ionic capitals, that flank the arcaded panel of the recessed upper part, conceal two secret drawers. The panels in the upper part are inlaid with geometrical patterns. The cornice is not original. (*In the Victoria and Albert Museum.*) The form of the press cupboard persisted throughout the 17th century; larger varieties are sometimes known as hall cupboards, and a late example is shown on page 86.

Early 17th century panelled room, with strapwork on the pilasters and plaster ceiling: from Bromley-by-Bow. *Now in the Victoria and Albert Museum*. The detail of the carved chimneypiece is shown opposite. The oak draw table in the centre, *circa* 1600, is inlaid with sycamore and bogwood; the oak dresser with the moulded drawer-fronts and split balusters on the front, is late 17th century, and the two joined chairs with panelled backs and scrolled cresting date from the second quarter of the century. The chair on the left, by the chimneypiece, with lunette ornament carved on the back below the cresting, and on the seat rail, is not in the Museum collection.

Detail of the chimneypiece in the Bromley-by-Bow room on the opposite page. Contemporary copy books, with their plates of architectural details and ornament, have influenced the character of the design; but despite the diversity of ornamental motifs, the composition is masterly; the proportions admirable, and horizontal and vertical elements are complementary. The significance of the classic orders as a system of design is beginning to be appreciated by English architects and craftsmen. The designs of Inigo Jones for masques and plays at the Court of James I, had enlarged the visual education of royal and noble patrons, and increased their familiarity with the subtleties of Renaissance architecture.

1595, and is an early example of a mule chest, a modern term for a joined chest with two or three drawers in the base.

During the second half of the 16th century furnishing was luxurious; the variety and convenience of individual articles of furniture increased, so did the competence of joiners, carvers and upholsterers. William Harrison in *The Description of England* observed that the houses of noblemen contained "abundance of Arras, rich hangings of Tapestrie, silver vessels, and so much other plate, as may furnish sundrie cupboards, to the summe ofentimes of a, thousand or two thousand pounds at the least. . . ." In the homes of knights, gentlemen and merchants there was also a "great profusion of tapistrie, Turkey worke, pewter, brass, fine linen, and thereto costly cupboards of plate, worth five or six hundred or a thousand pounds. . . ." Such lavish furnishing, "descended yet lower, even unto the inferior artificers, and manie farmers", who had "learned also to garnish their cupboards with plate, their (joined) beds with tapestrie and silk hangings, and their tables with carpets & fine naperie. . . ."

An improved and more compact version of the plate cupboard, with its tall desk for display and receptacles below, was introduced in the form of a sideboard with two open tiers, a pot board just above floor level, and sometimes a small, splay-sided central cupboard between the middle and upper tier. The contemporary name for this was a court cupboard, though it was also called a buffet. The examples on page 54 illustrate the basic form, which remained unchanged from the late 16th to the end of the 17th century. Another type for the display and storage of plate was the press cupboard, with ample accommodation below and a recessed superstructure above with smaller cupboards and a shelf in front of them. (See page 55.) Press cupboard is also a contemporary term, which was still in use in the early 18th century. The larger varieties are sometimes described as hall cupboards; but the term parlour cupboard, for the small, richly ornamented types, is not contemporary. Another form had an open pot board below, two tiers of cupboards above, and was on the same scale as the court cupboard.

The background for furniture might be provided by the "rich hangings of Tapestrie" that Harrison mentions, but in great country mansions and the comfortable and spacious town houses that were built in London and other cities, the walls of large and small rooms were often panelled in oak, with impressive chimneypieces carved in wood or moulded in plaster, and a ceiling of highly decorative plasterwork. The early 17th century room from a house in Bromley-by-Bow, now in the Victoria and Albert Museum, illus-

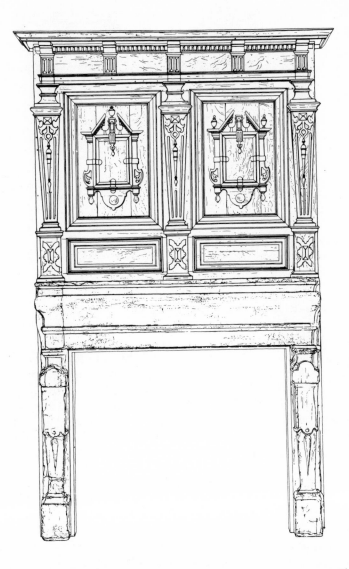

Chimneypiece formerly in a house in Lime Street, London. *Circa* 1620. The entablature of the upper part has some of the characteristics of the Doric order, with triglyphs in the frieze; but the tapering pilasters decorated with split balusters and strapwork and the ornamental composition in the panels, with broken pediments and urns (three of the urns are missing), are derived from contemporary copy books of architectural detail. *In the Victoria and Albert Museum.*

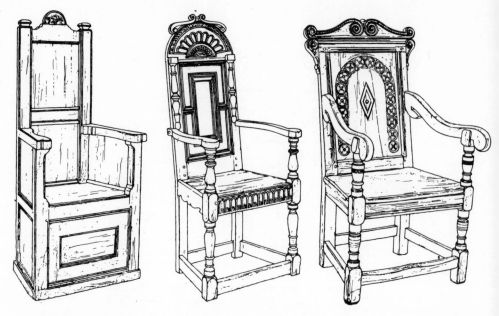

Left: Joined chair, with the date, 1574, carved in the lunette above the top rail. Structurally this box-like chair resembles the earlier example at the left of page 33. *In the Victoria and Albert Museum.*

Centre: Joined armchair of oak, with turned front legs and arm supports, a panelled back, arched head, with carved decoration and slender scrolled cresting; split balusters are applied to the back on each side of the panel. The date 1585 and the initials RW carved on the upper part of the back panel were added subsequent to the making of the chair, but the design suggests that it was made near that date. This is a simplified English version of the French conversation chair on page 46. *In the possession of the Society of Antiquaries of London, and reproduced by courtesy of the Executive Committee.*

Right: Joined armchair in oak with panelled back and scrolled cresting. Chairs of this type were made from the late 16th to the mid-17th century. *Formerly in the possession of Mrs Grace Lovat Fraser.*

Joint or joyned stool, with four turned legs, stretchers below and rails above that support a flat rectangular seat. The construction is the same as that used for the joined chair, *top right*. This is a mid-17th century example, for, apart from variations in the turning of the legs, the form remained unchanged from the 16th to the early 18th century. *In the author's possession.*

trated on page 56, is an example of highly finished joinery work, carried out by craftsmen who were acquiring a sensitive appreciation of the proportions of classic architecture. The chimneypiece, shown on page 57, is a masterly composition, brilliantly executed by highly accomplished carvers. The less ambitious chimneypiece on page 59, formerly in a house in Lime Street and also in the Victoria and Albert Museum, is a little later in date, but although indebted to contemporary copy books of architectural detail, with their own peculiar versions of antique ornament blended with strapwork, classic proportions have prevailed, and the entablature of the overmantel reproduces some of the characteristics of the Doric order.

Seat furniture was improved in design, though the rigid, flat-seated box-like chairs of the early 16th century continued in use, and one of these survivors, shown opposite, top left, has the date 1574 carved on the lunette cresting. Late in the century, joined chairs were introduced with turned arm supports and front legs, back legs and stretchers of square or rectangular section, and a slightly raked panelled back, like the examples in the interior on page 56 and opposite, top right. The panel was usually ornamented by incised carving or inlaid patterns. The basic form of such joined chairs remained unchanged from the late Elizabethan period until the reign of Charles II. A modern name for them is panel-back, which describes the structure; the contemporary name was wainscot chair, which describes the material, and was applicable to any solidly-constructed armchair. (The two planks cut from the centre of an oak log provided wainscot boards, and from the 14th to the mid-17th century the name wainscot meant oak.) The term armchair or "arming chair" was originally adopted to distinguish a chair with arms from a back stool. A graceful and lighter example of joined chair is shown opposite, top centre, with an arched head, slender scrolled cresting, and a recessed panel in the back, framed and decorated with mouldings of bold section. This is a modified version of the French conversation chair on page 46, and in common with other joined chairs of this period, the front legs and arm supports only are turned, unlike the French example that has four turned legs.

Folding stools and chairs had been used in Italy for at least a hundred and fifty years before a new and improved design was introduced in England during the second half of the 16th century. The type illustrated on page 63, top left, is the so-called "Glastonbury" chair, a term invented and popularised in the mid-19th century, when it was supposed to resemble a folding chair alleged to be the property of Richard Whiting, the last Abbot of Glaston-

61

bury, who was executed in 1539. (This legend probably arose from Sir Samuel Rush Meyrick's description of a folding chair illustrated on plate IX of Henry Shaw's *Specimens of Ancient Furniture*, published in book form in 1836.) Chairs with a folding frame could be stacked flat against a wall when not in use, and this type was made and used until the early 19th century. Another piece of folding furniture, introduced at the beginning of the 16th century and increasingly popular throughout the 17th, was a convertible armchair, that combined the functions of a seat and a table, known as a chair-table, table-chair, or table-chairwise; contemporary terms that frequently occur in inventories. This was a flat-seated joined chair with a circular or rectangular back hinged to swing over and rest horizontally on the arms, thus forming a small table.

Turners throughout the 16th century improved a style of chair-making that demonstrated their ability to make light, highly ornamental, but structurally sound armchairs. The triangular-seated turned chair on page 32, top left, foreshadows the later, more ornate type shown opposite, described as "turned all over", and made chiefly in East Anglia, the west country and Wales. The rectangular seat, more spacious than the triangular shape, was sunk slightly below the level of the surrounding framework to keep a loose cushion in place. The commonest form of seat was the joint or joyned stool, strongly constructed, with turned legs and stretchers, the frame held together by mortice and tenon joints, fixed by dowels without glue. A name that often appears in late 16th and early 17th century inventories is buffet stool, identified with the joint stool by the late R. W. Symonds who said: "no other type has survived in sufficient numbers, which would account for its so frequent mention". Contemporary evidence suggests that joint stools were also used as tables by children. Apart from variations in the character of the turned legs, such stools were made in much the same form from the mid-16th to the beginning of the 18th century. The example at the foot of page 60 is of mid-17th century origin. The joint stool was structurally superior to the earlier, board-ended type shown on page 29, and far more resistant to the rough usage to which such easily movable seats were subjected, especially in taverns, when they were hurled about during drunken brawls.

Joint stools and benches were used in English dining parlours until the back stool was introduced, probably from France, and in both countries a type with an upholstered seat and back brought another specialised trade into chair-making, that of the upholsterer, whose contribution to comfort had hitherto been confined to loose pad cushions for seats. Though back stools are

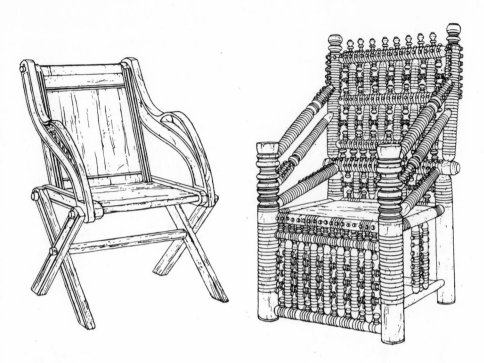

Left: Folding chair, late 16th century, the so-called "Glastonbury" type. *Right*: Turned chairs became far more elaborate during the second half of the 16th and the early part of the 17th century: in East Anglia, the west country and Wales, the skill of turners reached high levels, and such chairs were described as "turned all over". They remained in use in country districts for generations, and in 1761, Horace Walpole, who wanted to acquire some specimens, said: "They are of wood, the seats triangular, the back, arms, and legs loaded with turnery." The example above has a rectangular seat, but the earlier, triangular-seated types survived. *By permission of the National Museum of Wales, Welsh Folk Museum.*

mentioned in Elizabethan inventories, they were not in general use until the second quarter of the 17th century and did not rate as chairs, because they were armless, nor were they described as side or single chairs until much later. The two upholstered back stools on the next page, typical of those made during the first half of the 17th century, are sometimes called "farthingale chairs", not a contemporary name, and probably coined by some Victorian dealer or collector, who assumed that such broad-seated chairs were made to accommodate the wide, hooped farthingale, or fardingale, worn by women. The farthingale was a Spanish fashion, imported late in the 16th century, that became vastly exaggerated in the reign of James I, a great wheel of whalebone from which voluminous draperies depended, so that nobody wearing such enormous skirts could possibly sit in an armchair. The back stool was the only practical seat for women encumbered by such a fashion. A contemporary name for an armless chair with the seat and back stuffed and covered by fabric was imbrauderers' chair, another description was upholsterers' chair, for they were made in great quantities, sold by the dozen, and could be hired from upholsterers when additional seating was needed. They were made with small regional differences throughout Europe, sometimes plainly covered, sometimes with embroidered seats and backs. A wooden open-backed English type, made during the first half of the 17th century and shown below, is similar to the French example on page 46.

In many Elizabethan and Jacobean houses, upholstered furniture was not only luxurious, but comfortable. Comfort was an innovation, developed largely by the ingenuity of upholsterers. Chairs with broad, deeply-

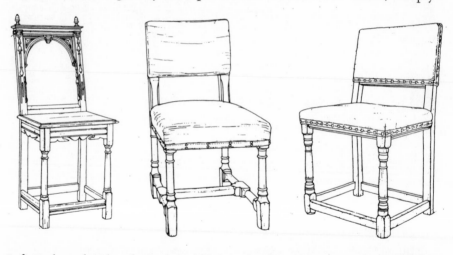

Left: Back stool with arched, open, slightly inclined back, with acorn finials decorating the top rail, and split balusters applied to the uprights. Early to mid-17th century. Compare with the open-backed late 16th century French example on page 46.
Centre and right: Upholstered back stools, first half of the 17th century. Armless chairs of this type were in use throughout Europe, with regional variations of turning for the legs. They have been called "Farthingale" chairs, which is not a contemporary term, though they were certainly used throughout the period when the farthingale was fashionable. They were also known as upholsterers' chairs, and were made throughout the 17th century; a contemporary name was imbrauderers' chair.

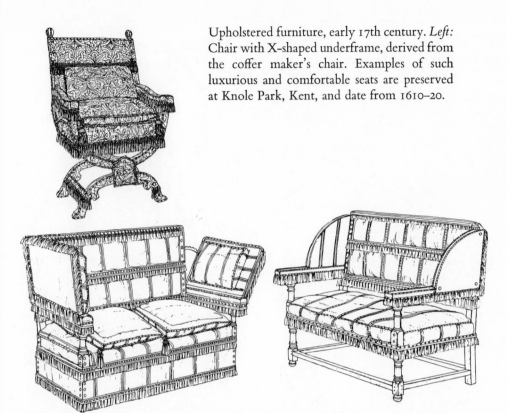

Upholstered furniture, early 17th century. *Left:* Chair with X-shaped underframe, derived from the coffer maker's chair. Examples of such luxurious and comfortable seats are preserved at Knole Park, Kent, and date from 1610–20.

Left: Sofa with adjustable side that, when lowered, transformed it into a day bed. *Right*: Upholstered settee, with wing pieces uniting arms and back. *Circa* 1620. Both based on drawings by Charles Locke Eastlake of furniture at Knole Park.

cushioned seats, X-shaped underframes, curved arm rests and gently sloping backs, followed the structural lines of the 15th and early 16th century coffer-makers' chairs, but with an amplitude and splendour that surpassed their forerunners. The underframing was covered in the same rich material used for the seat cushion and the back, brocade or coloured cloth embroidered with silk, or crimson velvet, trimmed with gallon and fringe and garnished with brass-headed, gilt nails, like a specimen at the Victoria and Albert Museum, *circa* 1610–20, which has a footstool to match. By the end of the 16th century settees with adjustable sides that could be lowered on metal ratchets to transform them into day-beds were made by upholsterers; the settee was a refined development of the 15th century settle depicted in contemporary manuscripts, broad enough to accommodate two or three people.

65

Right: Late 16th century folding table with turned legs and strapwork ornament. This example, drawn by F. W. Fairholt, is shown folded flat against a wall: when opened, the legs were pulled out, the one at the right having a projection at the top that fitted into a socket in the lion's mouth carved on the underside, where it was secured by a pin that hangs beside it. Reproduced from *A History of Domestic Manners and Sentiments in England,* by Thomas Wright (1862).

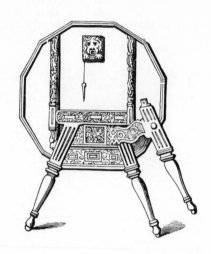

Left: Early 17th century gate-leg table with panelled ends. A compact and graceful design, sparingly ornamented, with double leaves resting on hinged supports when open. *In the Victoria and Albert Museum.*

In addition to draw tables like that illustrated on page 27, there were longer and more massive types with six or eight legs, for which the contemporary name was long table, not refectory table, which is modern dealers' jargon. Smaller tables were often constructed to save space, and crude folding varieties appeared in the 16th century, such as the example above drawn by Fairholt, inferior in design to the single and double drop-leaf tables in use during and after the Jacobean period.

The extravagant luxury of Jacobean furnishing had almost obliterated all traces of the native English style, when luxury was checked, and furniture design sobered by the unhappy Puritan period that darkened the middle decades of the 17th century.

SECTION 4. THE ÉBÉNISTES AND THE BAROQUE

From the late 16th century to the second quarter of the 17th, the development of a national style in France was arrested; the innovating, exploratory spirit of the Renaissance evaporated; social turmoil, the bitter legacy of political and religious wars, had unsettled the country, depleted creative inspiration, and debilitated the arts and crafts. Although Henry IV attempted to revive native industries, the workshops he established had to be staffed by Flemish and Italian craftsmen; meanwhile the Court and the few remaining wealthy patrons imported furniture and fabrics and ideas from abroad, from Italy, Spain, and the Low Countries, so foreign influences predominated in furnishing and interior decoration during his reign and after his assassination in 1610. In the period that followed, named after his successor Louis XIII, national character in design was reasserted, and furniture-making was revolutionised by the revival of the highly skilled craft of veneering, known and practised in Ancient Egypt, Greece and the Roman Empire, and rediscovered early in the 17th century, following the introduction of ebony, that heavy, smooth-grained, lustrous black wood, which did not shrink, warp or decay. Ebony changed established ideas about wood as a material; too hard and brittle to be used as woods were normally used, it was cut into veneers and laid on a flat surface. Presently thin sheets of other woods were applied to obtain decorative effects denied by solid material. The technique of laying veneers became the basis of cabinet-making in France, and because of its primary association with ebony the craft was called *ébénisterie* and a cabinet-maker an *ébéniste*.

Marquetry, closely associated with veneering, had developed from another ancient craft, that of inlaying one material into another; and the process of inlaying coloured woods, tortoiseshell, ivory, mother-of-pearl, scrolls and arabesques of gold, silver, copper, brass and pewter, into veneers, so that veneer and ornament formed one sheet, originated in Italy, and reached France by the beginning of the 17th century. Marquetry changed the character of ornament; carved and moulded detail was subordinated to surface decoration; and sparkling partnerships between gleaming metals and exotic woods and tortoiseshell were perfected later in the century by André-Charles Boulle

67

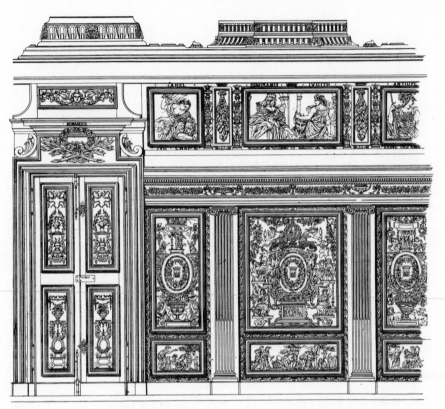

Interior design in the early part of the 17th century, regulated by classic proportions, and characterised by an orderly disposition of decorative panels on walls and doors, framed with mouldings of bold section. Compare the architrave and over-door in this example, with that on the opposite page. Oratoire cabinet de Sully.

(1642–1732), a great artist-craftsman whose name became a descriptive term for this form of decorative work.

Before the rise of the great *ébénistes* in the second half of the century, joiners and turners were developing and improving their complementary skills; the furniture they produced was strongly constructed without being ponderous; the strength was visible, but the angularity and rigidity inherited from mediaeval woodworkers melted away: hard lines were smoothed into modest

Door of the salon. Chateau de Cheverny. The scrolled grotesque on the overdoor, marked by Flemish influence, is an intrusive element in the composition, out of keeping with the delicately enriched architrave and cornice mouldings.

curves or broken by turned ornament. In seat furniture curvilinear design was foreshadowed, and on case furniture surfaces were varied by the use of fielded panels on drawer fronts and cupboard doors, with mouldings of bold section outlining the surrounding framework. By day, the sun, reaching through tall windows, emphasised high lights and drew shadows that hourly changed the character of every curve and facet; by night, inconstant candle flames were mirrored in the polished woodwork. Cupboards and buffets were still decorated with carving during the Henry IV period, though with less dependence on classical ornament, despite the increase of Italian influence on fashionable taste and the presence of Italian craftsmen in many workshops. Caryatides, atlantes and herms might adorn some upright members, but on panels and their frames naturalistic motifs were carved in low relief: flowers, fruit and stylised foliage, also trophies of arms. In great houses classical pro-

Details of furnishing shown in the engraving opposite. The walls are hung with tapestries: the tall casement windows uncurtained, with shutters folded back against the reveals. The proportions of the chimneypiece, the emphatic mouldings and boldly rendered ornament have survived from the early, vigorous phase of Renaissance design. Compare the vitality of this feature with the restrained and classically correct wall treatment on page 68. This early 17th century scene shows the homely comfort of a bourgeois household; a combined dining room, kitchen, and bedroom, with serviceable furniture. The chairs are a standard type, common throughout Western Europe in the 17th century, upholstered back stools, with the seats and backs trimmed with fringe and the upright back supports garnished with brass-headed nails. (See illustrations of the English variety on page 64.) The joined stool in the foreground, with turned legs and heavy, square-sectioned stretchers, has an upholstered seat, embroidered, with a line of brass-headed nails above the fringe. The table is probably a board on trestles, which are concealed by a heavy cloth, protected by a linen overcloth. The looking glass has a square, deep, moulded frame. The tester of the curtained bed has a deep valance, and urn-shaped finials above, probably covered in the same fabric as the bed curtains. In France, as in England, beds appeared in living rooms throughout the 17th century; but in France they were brought into decorative relationship with the rest of the furnishing: in England, they were there merely to provide additional sleeping accommodation when necessary.

Within the engraving, the following captions appear:

Joy viennent a la haste
Les Enfans de Mar dy gras
Mettre la main a la paste
Reformant a tour de bras.

La Cuisine les attire
Soit par coustume, ou par jeu,
Et les bignets les font rire
Tandis qu'ils sont pres du feu.

L'HYVER

Monsieur, dict vne Maistresse
Si vous touchez mon teton,
Je respandrey de la graisse
Sur vostre habit de Satin.

Mais cette picotterie
Je tromine incontinent,
Et toute leur raillerie
Est de Caresme-prenant.

Above: One of a series of four engravings of "The Seasons", by Abraham Bosse (1602–76), depicting an early 17th-century interior. The scene represents Winter, and all the indoor comforts of that season. (See opposite page for details of the furnishing.) *Reproduced by Courtesy of the Trustees of the British Museum.*

Right: Early 17th century flat-seated joined stool with turned baluster legs, slightly splayed, and a square-sectioned stretcher. Compare with the simpler frame of the upholstered stool in the engraving.

71

portions determined the character of interior decoration, as exemplified by the wall treatment on page 68, with panels separated by fluted Ionic pilasters. Panelled walls were painted with landscapes and scenes illustrating the exploits of Greek and Roman heroes and legends of the pagan gods, interspersed with floral compositions and intricate arabesques. In the spacious houses of the wealthy merchant and trading class, walls were hung with tapestry, or rich materials such as velvet and damask, like the interior depicted by Abraham Bosse, reproduced on page 71, where the chimney-piece alone suggests the influence of the Renaissance.

From the beginning to the end of the 17th century, turning was used extensively on furniture, especially in the Louis XIII period, appearing on the legs and stretchers of chairs, tables and cabinet stands. Decorative turning in France certainly owed something to the example of craftsmen in the Low Countries, though the spiral twist originated in Italy, and may have been inspired by some architectural prototype, such as the twisted columns of the baldacchino at St. Peter's, designed by Bernini and begun in 1625. Turners, working with a more tractable material than stone, refined the form of the twist, so that it enlivened the character of bedposts and chair frames, like the examples opposite, and the vertical members of the cupboard on page 74. Other ornamental forms were invented, ball, bobbin and ring turning, and later in the century the elegant trumpet-shaped leg was introduced, that rose from a moulded base or a bun foot and expanded as a slender, elongated cone. The trumpet leg probably originated in Holland, and was soon adopted by French and English craftsmen.

New technical methods and fashions in ornament crossed every frontier in 17th century Europe as they did in the Middle ages, though the application of methods and the interpretation of ornament bore the impress of national character; so when some fresh style arose in one country it was soon naturalised in others, and this happened with Baroque, the last dynamic style created in Italy. In architecture, Baroque restored depth to buildings; the flat, correct façades, regulated by proportions proper to one or other of the classic orders, were replaced by expressive compositions, sculptural in effect, and commanding the services of light and shade to dramatise the rediscovery of three dimensions. Externally and internally it was a sculptor's style; opulent, arrogantly ornamental, but dignified, and those characteristics were reflected by the design and embellishment of furniture during the Louis XIV period.

Before the Baroque style was established in France, large and luxurious apartments had been transformed by the increasing use of the suite, closely

related in design to the decorative treatment of the interior, thus bringing greater coherence to the art of furnishing. The suite consisted of matching chairs, stools, couches and settees; sometimes numbering as many as twenty-four chairs and stools, and two or four settees. In England, suites of upholstered chairs had been introduced in the latter part of Elizabeth I's reign; but the idea of unifying the design of various types of seat furniture was French.

The suite with its various components was designed for spacious rooms, for the galleries of great town houses, where works of art were exhibited, or the salons where aristocratic gatherings, arrayed in the latest fashions indulged their taste for polite conversation. In the less pretentious and far more comfortable rooms of bourgeois households, seat furniture consisted of back stools, like the standard type in the interior on page 71; there were also

Above: Two-tiered cupboard with four doors, and deeply-moulded, octagonal panels; the cupboards are divided and flanked by coupled columns, decorated by alternating spiral twists; the whole surmounted by a projecting cornice with dentils. That rather vague term, *armoire*, is sometimes used for such tall, mid-17th century cupboards; but they were in the process of transition from the four-doored cabinet to the two-doored press, to which name *armoire* is more correctly applied. This is an example of the decorative fecundity of the French cabinet-maker, who has invented the ornamental treatment, and merely touched his cap to classical details and proportions.

Opposite page: Another example of mid-17th century two-tiered cupboard, with the upper stage set back. Ball-turning is used to decorate the coupled columns on the vertical members, and like the more elaborate cupboard shown above, the decorative character of the design is derived from the skilful use of varied surfaces and heavy mouldings. The influence of classic ornament is asserted by the acanthus leaves carved on the modillions below the bases of the coupled columns. The cupboard is supported on bun feet recessed below the heavily moulded base.

74

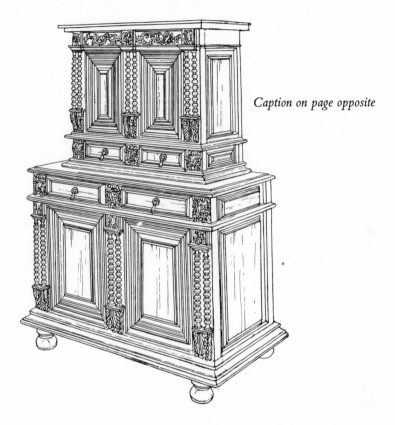

Caption on page opposite

joined armchairs with high backs, ponderous legs on ball feet and strong, square-sectioned stretchers. Chairs were the last articles to lose mediaeval angularity; even when legs, stretchers and arms were lightened by ball or spiral turning, rigidity of line persisted until late in the Louis XIII period. Joined stools with plain turned legs and flat wooden or upholstered seats were in general use in France as in England; two examples are shown on page 71, one in the interior by Abraham Bosse. The bedroom in 16th and 17th century France was an important apartment; in large houses it was also a reception room; in bourgeois homes, an all-purpose room, like that depicted by Bosse, with a bed, a trestle dining table, and a fireplace big enough to facilitate cooking.

New types of furniture appeared and old types changed their shape and enlarged their functions: the metamorphosis of the buffet is an example of such a change, for the two-tiered cupboard with four doors became a high cupboard with two, known as an *armoire*, an inexact term that also denoted an aumbry or any large press or two-doored cupboard. Such specialised articles as the bureau were introduced: though little more than a writing table with a couple of drawers when it first came into use, it became more commodious and decorative after the middle of the century. Small tables with turned legs and stretchers, and square, rectangular or oval tops contributed to the convenience of furnishing; solid pieces of joinery, but light enough to be easily moved. The massive, elaborately carved tables that supported slabs of ornamental marble, still appeared in great houses, and were developed from the late 16th century type, shown on page 47, strongly marked by Italian influence.

The age of magnificence, generated in the second quarter of the 17th century, reached its most expansive phase during the last three decades, reflecting the brilliancy and grandeur of that specialist in splendid extravagance, Louis XIV. But the splendour was solemn; enormously dignified; and the levity of the Rococo style was still three generations away.

Left: Armchair fitted with ratchet to lower the high back. Legs and arm supports have ring turning; a rising serpentine stretcher unites the legs above the bun feet. *Centre*: A later type of high-backed armchair with scrolled legs and curved stretchers. Compare with the still later designs by Marot on page 98. *Right*: Small table with drawer, turned legs and serpentine stretcher: such relatively simple types were made from the middle to the end of the 17th century.

SECTION 5. PURITAN AUSTERITY: CAROLEAN LUXURY

During the fourth, fifth and sixth decades of the 17th century the extreme simplicity of English furniture design and the frugal use of ornament reflected the austerity of the puritan period. To some extent, the native style of the late 15th and first half of the 16th century was resumed, though woodworkers were a hundred years better off in technical knowledge and far more accomplished than their predecessors who had followed the Gothic tradition. The influence of those often disastrous Flemish and German copy books diminished: their plates showing cobbled-up versions of classic motifs intermingled with strapwork were perhaps equated with royalist luxury; certainly they were ignored when the carver resumed his responsibility for ornament, uninhibited by any obligation to interpret the congested fancies of some foreign engraver who had never had a woodworking tool in his hands. Meanwhile the turner had become gaily inventive; his ornamental work showed that innocent light-heartedness could survive in the glum atmosphere of spiritual dictatorship; though such refinements as spiral turning, long familiar in France, were not employed until the end of the Commonwealth.

Seat furniture was no longer upholstered with richly embroidered fabrics; plain leather, garnished with brass-headed nails, covered the seats and backs of chairs and settees; ball and ring turning gave variety to legs and stretchers; but carved decoration was rationed and usually confined to the arched cresting of joined panel back chairs or the horizontal members that united the back uprights of single chairs. Hard, flat wooden seats were usual, as on the turned and joined example in walnut at the top of page 79, and the early 17th century form of back stool survived not only in the countryside but as an item of fashionable furnishing, when fashion came into its own again at the restoration.

Puritan taste—if it may be called taste at all—had a sobering effect on design; every seat, table, press and cupboard became a solemn statement of structural fact; the accumulations of carved ornament that adorned and sometimes defaced Jacobean furniture disappeared; proportions improved;

77

the interior environment of furnishing was changed; a new orderliness transformed the background; every line and detail of panelled rooms, walls, door and window architraves, disclosed a sensitive knowledge of classic architecture. Whereas the rooms of the early 17th century, with their vast chimney-pieces, suggested a classic building seen through distorting mist, clarity of shape was favoured when excessive ornamentation was certain to arouse the suspicion of the unco guid: one of the rare examples of moral censorship exercising a beneficent influence, though the puritan dictators would have shrunk from the idea that their incapacity for enjoyment was indirectly responsible for any form of artistic refinement. These changes were also attributable to the enlargement of architectural education, and increasing respect for Vitruvian rules, following the example of Inigo Jones, the father of English Renaissance architecture, whose interpretation of the classic orders had dispelled the discords and confusions of Elizabethan and Jacobean design. This period of architectural illumination, coinciding with a return to the basic structural simplicity of the native English style, gave an exceptional quality to the character of puritan furniture; a comfortable, reassuring quality, for the puritans, far from averse to comfort, were only selectively censorious. For example, children were allowed to smoke, but were forbidden plum pudding, and nobody thought strong drink was sinful if swallowed secretly at home, though gay clothes and upholstery were definitely identified with the unregenerate. But all these dark conflicts of belief, and the restrictions they begot, were blown away in 1660 when Charles II was restored to the throne, and the luxury trades to their former prosperity.

English makers, hitherto excluded from participation in the spirited innovations of Baroque, were at last able to celebrate their release from organised austerity by an exuberant interpretation of that style: the master carvers who ornamented furniture gave to acanthus foliations, naturalistic and heraldic motifs, and elongated S-scrolls, a jocund pliability. Chubby amorini, symbolising Carolean permissiveness and gaiety, perched seductively on the cresting and stretchers of chairs and day-beds, or sported amid the carved fruit and flowers on cabinet stands and tables; and everywhere those long S-scrolls, as ubiquitous as C-scrolls became in Rococo, foreshadowed the gracious triumphs of curvilinear design that revolutionised the character of furniture in England and France during the next half century. Within twenty years of the Restoration, puritan plainness was banished from the rooms of fashionable houses, though the bleak, sturdy shapes survived in furniture of the countryside until the mid-18th century. Rigidity of line remained, masked

78

Left: Flat-seated, turned and joined chair in walnut. *Circa* 1650. *Centre*: Back stool upholstered in leather and garnished with nails. *Circa* 1650–60. Decorative turning provides the only relief from prevailing austerity in furniture design. *Right*: Chair with spiral turning on legs, stretchers and back uprights; seat and back covered in embroidery and trimmed with decorative fringes. *Circa* 1660. The basic form of the early 17th century back stool is preserved; the embroidery proclaims the return of luxury. (See page 64.) *In the Victoria and Albert Museum.*

The gate-leg table with double leaves was enlarged in size and improved in design after the middle of the 17th century. *Left*: This example has turned legs and under-framing of applewood, leaves and top of oak. *In the possession of Mrs F. J. Custance.* *Right*: Later example, with the so-called "barley-sugar twist" on the legs. *Formerly in the possession of the late Fleetwood Pritchard, Esq.*

it is true by carved ornament, and in seat furniture lightened by the introduction of canework on the seats and backs of chairs. The cane chair-maker
was established as a specialist craftsman early in the sixteen sixties and met a
growing demand for relatively cheap, light and comfortable chairs; comfortable, because a flat caned seat and a slightly inclined caned back were yielding,
and diminished the angularity of a rigid frame. Soon upholsterers began their
long war against dignified posture which was artificially preserved by wig-
makers and hair-dressers for a hundred years after the easy chair was invented.
The high backs of Carolean and late 17th century chairs were related to
hairdressing fashions; the magnitude of the wigs worn by modish gentlemen
forbade lounging; both men and women sat bolt upright on chairs; the
day-bed was for reclining, and some chairs were made to allow the back to
be lowered on a ratchet, a device introduced early in the 17th century, but
improved during the Carolean period. The two "Sleeping Chayres" in Ham
House, Petersham, Surrey, *circa* 1675, are examples of this conspicuous concession to comfort. (One is shown opposite.)

The pleasure derived from visible heat, the hope of conserving the warmth
of a coal or wood fire, and the need for protection against currents of cold air
that penetrated English rooms, influenced makers of seat furniture, and the
high-backed settle with shaped end pieces that acted as draught-excluders,
was the model for the easy chair with lugs or wings, a type that Hepplewhite
called a "saddle cheek", and the late Victorians "a grandfather chair". By the
end of the century the basic shape of the winged easy chair was perfected:
thereafter it was varied only in the treatment of the legs and the shape of the
arms and wings: the original form remained unchanged for over two hundred
years. (The examples on pages 111, 142, and 196, illustrate this continuity of
design.) The tentative approach to curvilinear design marked by the introduction of the elongated S-scroll, was followed up by chair-makers who discovered that curves used in three dimensions gave a new and gracious character to the arms. Those on joined chairs had two-dimensional curves: now they
were curved in length, depth and width, as on the walnut armchair, *circa*
1690, on page 110.

In England as in France, the difference between furniture made for great
town houses and for small country homes became more marked in the
second half of the 17th century; fashionable cabinet-makers and carvers,
influenced by the baroque style and the mounting interest in oriental taste,
produced such opulent articles as the cabinet on page 83, japanned in gold,
silver, red and green on a black ground, and resting on a stand of carved and

Carolean gaiety was reflected by the exuberance of carved ornament: S-scrolls, acanthus foliations and naturalistic motifs were associated with turned members, and English makers, excluded from participation in the Baroque style by the Puritan régime, were at last able to experiment with the vigorous decoration that French craftsmen had tried out in the middle years of the 17th century. The examples, left and centre, illustrate the beginning of English Baroque. *Left*: Single chair in walnut with caned seat and back. *Circa* 1675. *Centre*: Carved and turned walnut armchair with scrolled front legs, arm supports and stretchers, and double S-scrolls used as vertical and horizontal decorative elements in the back. *Circa* 1670. *In the Victoria and Albert Museum. Right*: One of a pair of "Sleeping Chayres" at Ham House, Petersham, Surrey, with carved legs and front stretcher and spiral turning on the arm supports.

silvered pinewood. The stand, with its florid ornament, exemplifies the control carvers had begun to exercise over design, for the status of the carver had changed; he had become an independent craftsman, working in his own right, no longer a mere employee of cabinet-makers, joiners, or chair makers; he had also entered into a productive partnership with the gilder, so "carver and gilder" was established as a trade description that remained effective for nearly two hundred years. Greatest among the carvers whose work introduced a fresh and naturalistic note to the character of ornament, was Grinling Gibbons, discovered by John Evelyn in 1670, and described many years later by Horace Walpole, as a man "who gave to wood the loose and airy lightness of flowers, and chained together the various productions of the elements with the free disorder natural to each species" (*Anecdotes of Painting in England*). This master craftsman's gift for naturalistic carving was gracefully accommodated within the framework of classic composition.

Lime and such fruit woods as pear were chiefly used by carvers; the lime tree was known as the carver's tree, and Evelyn commended pearwood *"for its excellent colour'd* Timber, hard and levigable (*seldom or not ordinarily* worm-eaten) *especially for* Stools, Tables, Chairs, Pistol-Stocks, Instrument-Maker, Cabinets, *and very many works of the* Joyner (*who can make it easily to counterfeit* Eboney) *and* Sculptor, *either for* flat, *or* emboss'd-*Works, and to* Engrave *upon, because the* Grain *intercepts not the* Tool". (*Pomona*, an appendix to *Sylva*. Third edition, 1679. Chap. VIII, page 363.) The reference to counterfeiting ebony indicates how common the practice of dyeing and staining wood had become: and after John Stalker and George Parker published *A Treatise of Japaning and Varnishing* (Oxford: 1688), the staining, varnishing, gilding and lacquering of wood brought a new and lively decorative quality to furniture. The gilder flourished. An entry in Evelyn's *Diary* records a visit to "a gold-beater's work-house, where he showed me the wonderful ductility of that spreading and oily metal. He said it must be finer than the standard, such as was old angel-gold, and that of such he had once to the value of £100 stamped with the *agnus dei*. . . ." (September 19th, 1683.)

Candle-stand in silver; one of a pair that form part of a dressing table set. From Knole Park, Sevenoaks. Furniture of solid silver was rare; but the metal was simulated on carved decoration by the use of silver instead of gold leaf, as on the carved stand of the cabinet shown opposite.

Cabinet japanned in gold, silver, red and green on a black ground, supported on a carved and silvered pinewood stand. Last quarter of the 17th century. The bold, florid, carving of the stand has a robust vitality, though the figures with their protuberant stomachs emerging from acanthus foliations are coarse in treatment by contrast with the rest of the florid composition. The gilt brass mounts are not original. *In the Victoria and Albert Museum.*

Gilding was used extensively, not only to embellish the carved ornament on furniture, chimneypieces and overdoors, but on walls and upholstery. Almost immediately after the Restoration, Pepys has an entry that reads: "This morning my dining-room was finished with greene serge hanging and gilt leather, which is very handsome." (October 19th, 1660.) Leather was dyed and stamped or embossed with gilt patterns. Silvering, almost as popular as gilding, was applied by a similar process with silver leaf instead of gold, and appeared on cabinet stands (like the example on page 83), tables, and occasionally on the frames of looking glasses. More rarely solid silver was used, but little of that costly furniture has survived. It was too convenient as a financial reserve, too easily melted down. At Knole Park, Kent, a matching set of silver furniture for a dressing room, consists of a rectangular looking glass with a deep frame surmounted by intricate cresting; a table with a triangular apron piece below the frieze and scrolled legs; and a pair of candle-stands, supported on scrolled feet. (One of the candle-stands is shown on page 82.) This set, cast in solid metal, was made in the second quarter of the century. Pepys mentions a "great looking glass and toilet, of beaten and massive gold," presented to Catherine of Braganza, Charles II's Queen, by the Queen Mother and sent from France. (*Diary*, May 12th, 1662.) Evelyn's description of "the rich and splendid furniture" of the Duchess of Portsmouth in her apartment, "now twice or thrice pulled down and rebuilt to satisfy her prodigal and expensive pleasures", included "Japan cabinets, skreens, pendule

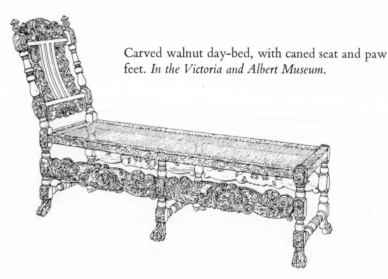

Carved walnut day-bed, with caned seat and paw feet. *In the Victoria and Albert Museum.*

The chimneypiece of the North Drawing Room, at Ham House, Petersham, Surrey. The plaster frieze and ceiling date from 1637; the twisted half columns, on either side of the fireplace, which may have been influenced by the work of the German artist, Francis Cleyn (1582–1658), are examples of the Baroque style, which had little opportunity of development in England until after the Restoration in 1660. *By courtesy of the Victoria and Albert Museum.*

85

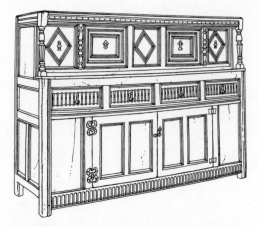

Left: Mid-17th century hall cupboard with extremely simple ornament: no carved decoration appears, and the sobriety of the native English style has been revived. These capacious variations of the press cupboard furnished the halls and large rooms of country houses. *Formerly in the possession of the late Fleetwood Pritchard, Esq. Right*: Mid-17th century joined chest of oak, with two drawers in the base. Massive, heavy, commodious, such chests, made throughout the puritan period, were the forerunners of more elaborate types. *In the author's possession.*

clocks, great vases of wrought plate, tables, stands, chimney-furniture, sconces, branches, braseras, &c., all of massy silver, and out of number. . . ." (October 4th, 1683.) Furniture of solid gold or silver was not exclusive to royalty and royal mistresses: the examples at Knole Park have been mentioned: there were many others. In a house belonging to the Earl of Chesterfield "the bride chamber which used to be call'd the Silver roome", had "stands table and fire utensils. . . . all massy silver", according to Celia Fiennes, who added: "when the plaite was in nomination to pay a tax, the Earle of Chesterfield sold it all and the plate of the house. . . ." (*The Journeys of Celia Fiennes*, part III, 1698.)

Mounts of silver and more rarely of gold adorned the work of cabinet-makers, and the chased door hinges on japanned cabinets were sometimes silver, more often of gilt brass. An ebony table with the legs modelled as caryatids, in Ham House, Petersham, Surrey, is "garnished with silver", and dates from the time when the house was enlarged and lavishly furnished by the Duke and Duchess of Lauderdale. The use of metal on furniture, almost bleakly functional before the 17th century, became far more sophisticated in the closing decades; new ornamental possibilities were recognised which contributed to the gaiety of design, but never descended to vulgarity, and were related tidily to the purpose of an article. The lines written by the Reverend Samuel Wesley in 1700, although concerning poetry, were applicable to the visual good manners of his time:

> "Style is the dress of thought; a modest dress,
> Neat, but not gaudy, will true critics please."

English furniture was neat, never gaudy, no matter how richly embellished. Style had been influenced by French taste throughout the reign of Charles II; French ideas were adopted, given a national flavour, and English makers rejected, or were perhaps unaware of, the impressive dignity of the Louis XIV style that had grown in grandeur as the political and artistic ambitions (and delusions) of the Sun King steadily expanded.

Surface variation and the decorative use of applied mouldings, characterised much of the case furniture in the third quarter of the 17th century; in France such treatments achieved a sumptuous effect although the ornamental

Left: Oak chest of drawers, veneered with palisander and ebony, the drawer fronts fielded and decorated with applied mouldings. *Circa 1660–80. In the Victoria and Albert Museum. Right*: Walnut chest on stand with oysterwood veneers. Crossbanding is used for bordering the top, panels and drawer front. *Formerly in the possession of the late Robert Atkinson, F.R.I.B.A.*

87

Left: Side table in oak with bobbin-turned legs and spiral turning on the stretchers. *Right*: Side table in oak with ball turning on legs and stretchers. *Circa* 1660–70.

components were relatively simple, as on the two-tiered cupboard on page 74; but compare that piece of French cabinet-making with the subdued richness of the fielded panels and moulded detail on the English chest of drawers on the lower part of page 87. The legacy of the Puritan period, with its enforced sobriety, is clearly proclaimed. The extreme simplicity of the applied mouldings on the upper stage of the hall cupboard on page 86 is an earlier example of Puritan restraint; but the chest of drawers, with its veneers of ebony and palisander is altogether different in design and execution: it is the work of a cabinet-maker, an accomplished craftsman who practised the technique of veneering; a sense of style has emerged; the dentil course below the top with the three shallow upper drawers that simulate a frieze, respectfully acknowledge the proportions and ornamental conventions of classic architecture. Since the second quarter of the century, turners had adapted the columns of the Doric and Tuscan orders for legs on tables and chairs; the stand that supports the walnut chest on page 106, top left, shows this use of the Tuscan column; cabinet-makers borrowed freely from the orders and the walnut scrutoire on page 107 reproduces an Ionic cornice moulding and pulvinated frieze.

Inevitably the magnificence of contemporary architecture influenced all woodworkers, and because it also attracted the alert and informed interest of the nobility and gentry, an age of educated patronage was gradually established when furniture was chosen for merit of design; such critical appraisal

Late 17th century settle with high panelled back and arms. The protective side pieces have been discarded: they were retained only on settles in the large kitchen fireplaces of inns and farmhouses. Usually such settles had cupboards or a locker below the seat. The arms on their turned supports are identical with those used on joined chairs in the first half of the century. (See page 60, top right.)

Low-backed settle, with carved top rail and stretcher, flat wooden seat, and turned arm supports and front legs. Like the high-backed example, the arms are of a type unchanged since the late 16th century. Settles of this type were introduced in the last quarter of the 17th century, and continued in use, with variations of detail, throughout the opening decades of the 18th, and were generally the work of country makers. *In the possession of John Atkinson, Esq., F.R.I.B.A.*

was very different from the haphazard acquisition of rich things by rich men, kings' doxies on the make, or collectors with a flair for exhibitionism, like the *malade imaginaire* satirised by Charles Cotton in his *Epigram de Mons. Maynard.*

Anthony feigns him Sick of late,
   Only to shew how he at home,
Lies in a Princely Bed of State,
   And in a nobly furnish'd Room
Adorned with pictures of Vandike's,
   A pair of Chrystal Candlesticks,
Rich Carpets, Quilts, the Devil, and all:
   Then you, his careful Friends if ever
You wish to cure him of his Fever,
   Go lodge him in the Hospital.

In France the reception of one's friends in a bedroom was normal social practice: in England the bedroom was a strictly private place, invaded only when a bride and bridegroom were "bedded down" by wedding guests. In some old-fashioned country manors and farm houses a bed might be included in the furnishing of a hall, to accommodate some chance visitor. In the great houses of the second half of the 17th century, state beds towered up to within a few inches of the lofty ceilings, with vast curtains and an elaborate tester. Above the corners of the tester urn-shaped finials sprouted tall plumes. From such beds, the carved wooden posts and headboard had disappeared: the head, like the tester and finials, was covered in the same material as the curtains. In the bedrooms of smaller houses, the fourposter was still in use, also the half-tester, and a variation of the latter type, known as an "angel-bed", with a diminished canopy projecting from the head, and barely covering the area occupied by the pillows.

French, and to a lesser extent, Spanish and Portuguese taste had affected Carolean design; Dutch influence came later, in the reign of William and Mary, and by the end of the century the curvilinear revolution that originated in Holland was beginning to change the shape and character of seat and case furniture.

SECTION 6. THE MAGNIFICENT STYLE

Magnificence and dignity distinguished the style of Louis XIV. The French king, a specialist in both regal qualities, was a lavish and ambitious patron, and the gifted architects, artists and craftsmen who worked for him fused the complexities and elaborations of Baroque into a controlled flamboyance. The whole art of furnishing was changed; a plastic quality was conferred on the design of furniture, and a new relationship established with the classic orders and their ornamental conventions. On walls and case furniture columns gave place to pilasters; the expressive forms of great Baroque buildings were discernible on a reduced scale in monumental cabinets, commodes, tables and looking glass frames; such splendid ornamental compositions often suggested architecture seen through a diminishing glass, for architectural design exerted a dominance over all the ancillary arts and crafts, and the architects who interpreted the taste of the King and the Court gave form and order to the fashions. In 1682 the Court was installed at Versailles, and the glamour of that prodigal palace excited the admiration of Europe. Jules-Hardouin Mansart transformed the exterior; Le Nôtre laid out the gardens; and Le Brun's treatment of the halls and salons transmuted Baroque into a national style, passionately luxurious and unequivocally French.

The style was animated by a fresh interpretation of the classic orders and a new understanding of the variety and possibilities of antique ornament; furniture was decorated with lively and original compositions, invented by designers and engravers like Jean Bérain (1638–1711), who mingled delicate arabesques with classical motifs, the inevitable acanthus foliations, wreaths, festoons, swags and slender scrolls. Bérain's designs certainly influenced many of the great *ébénistes*, like André-Charles Boulle; and his influence is apparent in the treatment of the writing table on page 96. Marquetry of tortoiseshell, brass, silver, pewter, mother of pearl and lapis lazuli gave those flexuous designs a sparkling, jewelled effect, surpassing in brilliancy all other forms of surface decoration. Although these materials had been used during the first half of the 17th century, Boulle, as mentioned in Section 4, used them with such transcendent skill that his name has ever since been associated with that form of intricate, partly metallic marquetry. Coloured woods were also

A Paris chez P. Mariette rue S.ᵗ Jacques a l'esperance   2

Interior of a salon with lofty door and window openings. This shows the controlling influence of classical architecture on the decorative background of late 17th century French furnishing. From Jean Le Pautre's book of designs. (See opposite.) *Reproduced by courtesy of the Victoria and Albert Museum.*

A plate from Jean Le Pautre's book of designs for console tables and looking glass frames. The table is flanked by a pair of *torchères*. The ornament is vigorously carved, the details admirably composed, and the motifs assembled without conflict. All the carved work would have been gilded, giving a rich, but not overpoweringly rich, effect. *Reproduced by courtesy of the Victoria and Albert Museum.*

93

Two commodes, designed by Jean Bérain, with classical motifs and delicate arabesques associated. *Reproduced by courtesy of the Victoria and Albert Museum.*

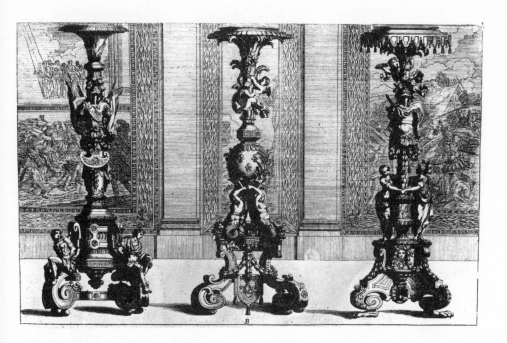

Three torchères, two of them with trophies of armour and weapons. Designed by Jean Bérain. (See previous page.) *Reproduced by courtesy of the Victoria and Albert Museum.*

used to form ornamental patterns; and the ebony veneers that had given the name *ébénisterie* to the craft of cabinet-making were replaced by veneers cut from rare and exotic timbers. As in contemporary England, the use of gilding and silvering became popular, and some furniture of solid silver was made, though almost exclusively for royal use.

The influence of Bérain's engraved designs on the decoration of furniture lasted until the opening decade of the 18th century. Earlier in Louis XIV's reign another designer and engraver, Jean Le Pautre (1618–82), had revivified antique ornament and given a new look to classical motifs and new, provocative life to the grotesques and herms, the griffins, sphinxes, winged leopards, sea-horses, centaurs, satyrs, and other fabulous hybrids of the Graeco-Roman world. Mingled with such ancient fantasies were the leaves of oak, laurel and acanthus, fruit and blossoms, scallop shells, human and animal masks, trophies of Roman armour and weapons; and those ever-present

95

Writing table by André-Charles Boulle. The influence of Bérain's designs is disclosed by the intricate arabesques and the general decorative character.

reminders of the power and glory of Royal Big Brother: the *fleur-de-lys*, the sunburst device, symbolising *Le Roi-Soleil*, and the king's personal cypher in the form of two L's, intertwined.

Charles Le Brun had brought furniture and interior decoration into a closer relationship, so that panelled walls, alcoves, chimney-pieces, the draperies of tall windows and beds and the carved ornament of furniture became components of an imposing, concordant scheme. The felicitous unity of design that resulted was revealed by Le Pautre's engravings. The scale of the vast galleries and rooms at Versailles and in the great houses of wealthy noblemen moderated the individual richness of carved and gilded furniture; detached from their original environment the decoration of many of those cabinets, commodes and tables, seems excessive, though absolved from vulgar ostentation by their dignified proportions and superlative workmanship. Jean Le Pautre's book of designs for console tables and looking-glass frames illustrates his easy mastery of ancient ornament; and the engraving on page

The almost overpowering magnificence of the Louis XIV style is expressed by this carved and gilt commode with elaborate metal inlay; despite the ornamentalists' exuberant work, the design has a coherent, controlled elegance, typical of the furniture that adorned the galleries and salons of Versailles.

93 is an example of sedate grandeur. When such designs were carved and gilt, they had a radiant splendour, impressive but never overpowering.

Upholsterers supplemented the work of carvers by giving a sculptural character to draperies; frills and double frills, ruching, pleating, braids and fringes allowed the valances of bed canopies, the lambrequins that filled window heads and masked the top of the curtains, and the curtains themselves to introduce a new dimension to interiors. The rich fabrics employed were not static decorative forms; they had a perceptible, tremulous life of their own, gently responsive to the unhurried movements and gestures of the brilliant company that thronged the salons and galleries. The significant rôle of fabrics in the development of the Louis XIV style is portrayed by the work of Daniel Marot (1663–1752), architect, engraver and furniture designer, whose father, Jean Marot (1620–79) was also an architect and engraver. Marot

98

Daniel Marot's designs for upholstered chairs, stools, bed valances and window pelmets. Reproduced from *Oeuvres du Sieur D. Marot*, published in Amsterdam: on the title page the author is described as "Architect de Guillaume iii, Roy de la Grande-Bretagne". The book was issued early in the 18th century, but many of the plates appeared in the last decade of the 17th in separate parts. Marot's baroque designs amalgamate Dutch and French influences, and strongly resemble English chairs of the William and Mary period. He visited London between 1694 and 1698. *Reproduced by courtesy of the Victoria and Albert Museum.*

99

State bed designed by Daniel Marot, reproduced from the same work as the previous plate. Marot's beds illustrate the growing importance of the upholsterer, for they are intricate compositions of carved decoration and drapery, with drapery as the predominant decorative element. In this example, the vast projecting tester, cantilevered forward from the headboard, and unsupported by front posts, is surmounted by urns at the corners with plumes above them. *Reproduced by courtesy of the Victoria and Albert Museum.*

Bedroom interior, Chateau de Wideville (Seine-et-Oise). Alcoves to accommodate beds, curtained and designed to relate them to the general decorative treatment, were a feature of many French bedrooms. The high-backed chair with padded arms and scrolled legs is almost identical with the design by Marot, centre left on page 98. Both the chair and commode suggest the growing influence of the curvilinear revolution on the shape of furniture.

was a Huguenot, born in Paris, but prudent enough to leave France before the King's disastrous Revocation of the Edict of Nantes. He settled in Holland and entered the service of the Stadtholder, who, when he replaced James II as King of England, appointed Marot as one of his consulting architects and Master of the Works. A folio volume of his designs for furniture and interior architecture, published in Amsterdam, was entitled *Oeuvres du Sieur D. Marot*: on the title page he described himself as "Architect de Guillaume iii, Roy de la Grande-Bretagne". His engravings strongly influenced English taste in the late 17th and early 18th century, and introduced some French and

Dutch characteristics to chairs and stools. The enhanced importance of the upholsterer is illustrated by Marot's designs for bedsteads, with their intricate draperies and huge projecting testers, unsupported by front posts, but cantilevered out from the tall headboard, and enriched by carved ornament covered with damask or velvet.

In France, as in England, upholsterers refined the shape and increased the comfort of seat furniture. Stiff angular chairs were replaced by designs that showed the impact of the curvilinear revolution which first affected the shape of legs and underframing and the line of the arm rests. The beginning of this change was apparent after the mid-17th century, and the chairs on page 76 represent an early development of curvilinear design. Before the end of the century chair seats were lowered in height, amplified in width and depth, and the backs raised: the winged armchair was introduced, though French makers avoided the frank concession to relaxation exemplified by the English easy

Two examples of late baroque. *Below:* Small side table with scrolled legs and stretcher, carved and gilt. *Right:* Single chair with heavily carved front legs and stretchers. Compare with Carolean chair on page 81.

Louis XIV day-bed, carved and gilt, with scrolled, rising stretchers. There is a similar example in the Musée des Arts Decoratifs, Paris.

chair. The high-backed armchair in the bedroom, page 100, has scrolled legs that are close to the cabriole form, and the Baroque chair with the caned seat and back on page 101 illustrates another variation of scrolled front leg, heavily masked by carved decoration, the whole design resembling a Carolean chair, though not so light: this French example is rather overloaded with carving.

The decoration of furniture and the character of furnishing were subjected to influences other than those supplied by the ancient world: the treasury of Roman and Greek ornament was never forgotten or long neglected, but in the second half of the 17th century classical motifs were supplemented by oriental ideas. In 1664 Jean Baptiste Colbert (1619–83) was appointed *Surintendant des Bâtiments*, and in that year he founded the *Compagnie des Indes Orientales*, which was intended to develop trade relations with China; but nearly all imports from the Far East reached France via Holland. Imported lacquer cabinets were mounted, as in England, on richly carved stands of wood, gilded or silvered; though such exotic articles were fashionable, the Chinese taste made little mark on furnishing until a relaxation of the dignity and discipline of the Louis XIV style was followed by the rise of Rococo.

Colbert established an Academy of Architecture; organised the work of cabinet-makers, carvers and tapestry-weavers; and created royal manufactories that were largely concerned with the furnishing and embellishment of the Palace of Versailles. The effect of his far-sighted policy is described in section 8, but an early result of the state's encouragement of manufactures was the expansion of the French glass industry following the invention of plate glass in 1687 by Bernard Perrot. The process that enabled large plates of perfectly flat polished glass to be produced made it possible to clothe large surfaces of wall with mirrors and, by the skilled manipulation of reflections, to give a majestic, albeit an illusory, spaciousness to interiors and to double the power of artificial lighting.

Although the style of Louis XIV is usually judged by the accomplishments of the great *ébénistes* and ornamentalists who served the Court, a more subdued version of it existed in the work of provincial makers, whose furniture, soundly constructed of local materials, was well-porportioned and sparingly embellished. Such craftsmen were under no obligation to cater for royal and aristocratic taste; they worked without reference to the engraved plates that had so consistently asserted the supremacy of the studio over the workshop, the drawing board over the bench, and they preserved the spontaneous ideas of past generations of woodworkers; consequently furniture of early and mid-17th century design was still being made long after the reign of Louis XIV was over. Even in the work of fashionable makers, the phases of the style overlapped, but the monumental character remained throughout the whole period of stifling grandeur and furious luxury.

Oak console, carved and gilt, with grotesque masks on the supports and apron. This late Louis XIV design with its flowing curves foreshadows the Rococo style. A comparable example is in the Musée des Arts Decoratifs, Paris. Compare with Pineau's designs on page 119.

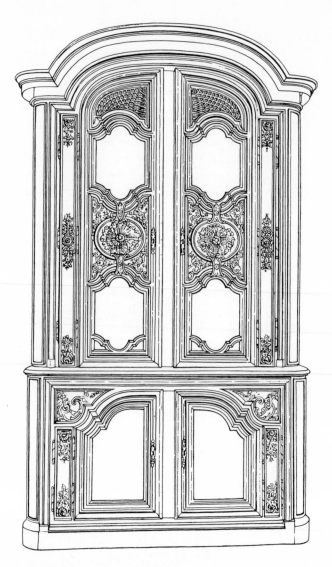

Oak cabinet with carved panels and pilasters and heavy mouldings. This early
18th century design retains some of the characteristics of mid-17th century work,
particularly in the use of moulded detail of bold section; but the carved ornament
has a delicacy that is incompatible with the emphatic form of the panels. The interlaced C-scrolls in the spandrels above the cupboards in the lower part suggest that
the carver had been influenced by the first, tentative and exploratory manifestations
of the rococo style. A cabinet of this type is in the Musée des Arts Decoratifs, Paris.

SECTION 7. THE WILLIAM AND MARY AND QUEEN ANNE STYLES

In England, as in France, the direction of craftsmen by professional designers became an established practice in the closing decades of the 17th century. In the countryside, rural craftsmen and the joiners and carpenters on the staff of great estates, retained much of their independence, followed traditional methods and perpetuated traditional forms, though skilled estate craftsmen were required by their employers to be familiar with the rules and proportions of the classic orders and the correct rendering and placing of classic ornament. In London and some of the larger provincial cities, the fashions were set by architects and their patrons, cultivated men of taste, whose ideas of design were seldom inordinate: overpowering magnificence has never appealed to English eyes. There were some exceptions amongst the nobility, but generally the modest desires of educated gentlemen resembled those condensed into a few lines of a poem called "The Choice", by John Pomfret (1667–1702), who wrote:

> Near some fair town I'd have a private seat,
> Built uniform; not little, nor too great;
> Better if on a rising ground it stood,
> On this side fields; on that a neighb'ring wood:
> It should within no other things contain
> But what are useful, necessary, plain:
> Methinks 'tis nauseous, and I'd ne'er endure
> The needless pomp of gaudy furniture.

That was written in 1700, the year Samuel Wesley had coined the phrase, "Neat, but not gaudy". Both writers were clergymen; both voiced respect for restraint and sobriety in the art of living; though such respect had nothing in common with the doleful repressions of Puritanism. A down-to-earth sagacity inclined English taste to moderation; Carolean profusion and excessive luxury had represented reaction against everything the puritans stood for; but even so, ornate furnishing had been largely confined to the Court and to the country seats and town houses of a few rich aristocrats who moved in

Two chests that illustrate the transition from rectilinear to curvilinear design. *Left*: Chest of drawers on stand, decorated with floral marquetry of walnut and other woods. The legs, which have been renewed, are turned to represent Doric columns. *Circa* 1690–1700. *Right*: Chest on stand, *circa* 1715–20. A forerunner of the double chest or tallboy. One long drawer and two smaller drawers are in the stand, which is supported on cabriole legs with carved shell ornament on the knees, and claw-and-ball feet below, the inset claws of ivory. Fluted quarter columns of the Corinthian order appear at the angles of the upper part. Richly-figured walnut veneer is used on oak and pine. *Both examples are in the Victoria and Albert Museum.*

Court circles, like the Duke and Duchess of Lauderdale, who furnished and decorated Ham House at Petersham in Surrey with the splendour of a royal palace. (See pages 81 and 85.)

Changes in the form and decoration of furniture followed the brief reign of James II. The William and Mary period was the prelude to an age of expansion; French and Dutch ideas had been absorbed and anglicised, and the growing influence of Dutch taste, beneficently pervasive, fostered a new and subtle appreciation of curves. During the last ten years of the 17th century the transition from the rigidity of high-backed chairs and emphatically rectangular chests and cabinets to the graces of curvilinear design was as significant as the change in contemporary domestic architecture that followed the introduction and general adoption of the double-hung sash window, which altered the proportions of rooms and increased the amount of daylight they received. The small rectangular panels, framed in series by stiles and rails, that had, since the late 15th century, usually covered walls from skirting to frieze, were superseded; the proportions were changed; the fielded panel provided surface variation; bold, bolection mouldings covered the joints between panel and frame, emphasising the different levels, and enriching walls with a pattern of lightly-drawn shadows. These orderly interiors, with their gentle gradations of moulded detail, reflected the calm dignity of the secular and sacred buildings that were arising in London and other cities. Furniture of the William and Mary period, though exhibiting the fading traces of mediaeval stiffness, had gracious lines, accentuated by a restrained use of carved ornament. Such sparing use of ornament announced very clearly that the first,

Late 17th century scrutoire, veneered in walnut, shown closed and open. The profile of the cornice and pulvinated frieze is correctly reproduced from the Ionic order. *In the possession of Mrs John Atkinson.*

107

Left: Chest of drawers in walnut, inlaid with lines of boxwood on the drawer fronts. The chest stands on bun feet. *Circa* 1690–5. *Right*: Early 18th century escritoire in figured walnut, with kneehole and cupboard behind. *Escritoire in the possession of Mrs John Atkinson.*

florid phase of the English Baroque style had ended. By the beginning of the 18th century, the part played by scrolls in Carolean seat furniture, tables and cabinet stands, was amplified; a new, curvilinear conception of design changed the form of seats and cabinets, and the introduction of the cabriole leg disclosed the variety and elegance of opposing curves. Although the angularities of chairs and cabinets survived throughout the William and Mary period, they were modified by the impact of the curvilinear revolution that determined the character of English furniture styles during the opening decades of the 18th century as, a hundred years later, a comparable revolution in the use of curves helped to form the character of the Regency style.

New materials were introduced; the use of such familiar woods as walnut was extended, thus following the recommendation of John Evelyn who, in his *Sylva*, had said: "were this Timber in greater plenty amongst us, we should have far better *Utensils* of all sorts in our Houses, as *Chairs*, *Stools*, *Bedsteads*, *Tables*, *Wainscot*, *Cabinets*, *&c.* instead of the more vulgar *Beech*, subject to the *worm*, weak, and unsightly; but which to counterfeit, and deceive the unwary, they wash over with a *decoction* made of *Green husks* of

Left: Table in elm, with single drop leaf and turned legs. *Right*: Side table in walnut, with spiral turning on legs, shaped stretcher, bun feet and inlaid marquetry decoration on the drawer front. *In the Victoria and Albert Museum.*

Walnuts, &c." (Quoted from the third edition, 1679, Chap. VIII, page 48.) Despite his strictures on the quality of beech, Evelyn recorded a range of uses for it, including dishes, trays, trenchers and dressing-boards, and stated that it was used by the "*Upholster* for *Sellyes, Chairs, Stools, Bedsteads*, &c." (Chap. V, page 38.) Sellye, selour or sellore, was a mediaeval term for the head of a bed, still current in the 17th and early 18th centuries, and as bed heads were generally covered with fabric to match the tester and curtains, they were classed as upholsterers' work. Beech when used for chairs, stools and settees, was usually painted.

Draw table in oak, with legs turned to simulate Tuscan columns, shown closed and with both leaves extended. Second quarter of the 17th century. *In the possession of John Atkinson Esq., F.R.I.B.A.*

Left: High-backed walnut single chair, with caned seat and back, arched front stretcher, and scrolls on the front legs. William and Mary period. *Victoria and Albert Museum. Centre*: Japanned chair, with scrolls at the junction of legs and seat rail and on the back. One of a set of seven in the Blue Drawing Room at Ham House, Petersham. *Right*: Walnut armchair, with scrolled arms and front legs. *Circa* 1690.

Evelyn recommended Virginian walnut, a much darker variety of the wood, that grew in the North American colonies. He also praised walnut imported from Grenoble, "of all other the most beautiful and esteemed". Comparatively little home-grown walnut was used; it was a poor wood constructionally, and the increasing amount of the material used during the late 17th century came from France and Italy, and after 1720 Evelyn's advice was followed and Virginian walnut extensively imported. Although this richly-figured, golden-coloured wood was used by cabinet-makers for a great variety of furniture during the first third of the 18th century, it was not a new or novel material. Walnut furniture is mentioned in late 16th and early 17th century inventories, and the wood was used concurrently with mahogany from the second quarter of the 18th century to the close of the Victorian period. That familiar but dubious description, "The Age of Walnut", has been identified with the Queen Anne style ever since it was first used by

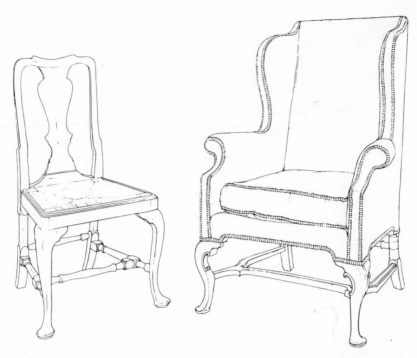

Left: Queen Anne bended back chair in walnut, with cabriole front legs and rush seat. *In the author's possession. Right*: Easy chair with wings, and walnut underframe. This became the basic form of winged armchair, which persisted throughout the 18th century. *Circa* 1700. *Victoria and Albert Museum.* Compare with examples on pages 142 and 196.

Percy Macquoid, as the title of the second volume of *A History of English Furniture* (1904–08). Few materials create a style, though a material or a process may become associated with some well-marked phase of furniture design. An exception, perhaps, is *papier-mâché*, that became a material in its own right in the mid-19th century and was instrumental in creating a light, elegant, highly ornamental style. Materials like gesso have contributed to the decorative development of a style. Both *papier-mâché* and gesso are inorganic compositions: no particular wood has ever initiated a style: its use has been determined by availability, occasionally decreed by a fashion, and maintained by convenience if it is a structural rather than a purely decorative wood. Processes have sometimes accelerated the growth and popularity of some fashions in furniture, as japanning accelerated the spread of the "Chinese Taste" in the late 17th century and helped to rejuvenate it forty years later. Although the graceful curves and classical proportions of Queen Anne furniture were often

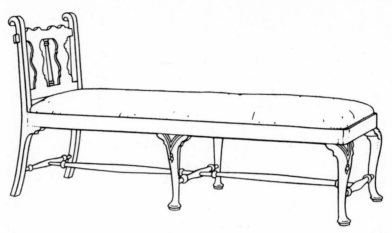

Day-bed in walnut, *circa* 1715. The head is adjustable and has two vase-shaped splats separated by a turned baluster; the uprights continue the line of the slightly splayed legs, and terminate in scrolls. The four cabriole legs have lightly carved ornament on the knees and rest on a club foot with a pad below. *Victoria and Albert Museum.*

expressed in walnut, many other woods were used, especially oak, which never lost favour with country craftsmen, also beech, yew and elm, and the various fruit woods, apple, plum, cherry and pearwood.

The technique of upholstery was progressively improved, and by the end of the 17th century the stuffing and padding of seats and backs had become an integral part of chair-making. A new specialist craftsman, known as a bed joiner, was employed by upholsterers to make the frames of beds, easy chairs and settees, and this gave upholsterers an ascendancy in the control of shape and style that they retained until the present century. With the development of the winged easy chair, the low-backed type, and the settee, seat, back, arms and sides presented a continuous fabric-covered surface, with wood showing only in the legs and underframing and perhaps the seat rail. The winged easy chair, *circa* 1700, on page 111, illustrates the preponderance of fabric, and this particular example, which is in the Victoria and Albert Museum, has a walnut underframe, with the back, roll-over arms, seat frame and cushion in gros-point and petit-point embroidery. (This is not shown in the drawing.) Makers began to dispense with underframing; the stretcher was discarded, and disappeared not only from some chairs and settees, but from tables. The bended-back chair with the gently curved splat and top rail, shaped like a milkmaid's yoke, was introduced, a modified version of a

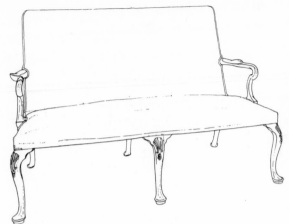

Walnut settee with cabriole legs terminating in club feet on pad bases, and shepherd's crook arms. The ornament is limited to lightly carved shells on the knees. First decade of the 18th century. *In the Victoria and Albert Museum.*

Chinese prototype, though unrelated to the Chinese taste. (See page 111.) The lines of the back and the cabriole legs and scroll-over arms gave these chairs an easy grace of shape and allowed those who used them to sit in a relaxed, comfortable manner, while the gentle inclination of the back discouraged any attitude that might have disturbed the set of a wig, the hang of a coat, or the billowing spread of skirts expanded by wide hoops.

The variety and convenience of furniture increased. Such articles as the bureau with a hinged writing space or flap appeared, the bureau surmounted by a cabinet or bookcase, the "desk and bookcase" as it was named in the mid-18th century; the knee-hole writing table; and the double chest or tall-boy. The dresser with a superstructure of shelves and cupboards, and the side-board table with an inlaid or a marble top, improved the amenities of dining rooms. Looking glasses in deep moulded or flat veneered frames reflected urbane interiors; sconces for single, double, or triple lights often had back plates of polished metal or mirror to increase candle-power; chandeliers depended from ceilings, with anything from four to eight branches, in brass or carved and gilded wood.

The national style, perfected during the reign of Anne, was both graceful and robust. The great age of English cabinet-making began.

Left: Bureau cabinet, veneered with burr walnut. *Circa* 1710–20. This became the basic form of the bureau-bookcase, or "desk and bookcase" as it was called in the 18th century.

Below: Chest of drawers with folding top that rests on sliding rails pulled out from either side of the top drawer. The chest rests on bracket feet. Walnut veneer on an oak carcase. First quarter of the 18th century.

Both examples in the Victoria and Albert Museum.

SECTION 8. THE ROCOCCO STYLE

From the early decades of the 18th century until the Revolution, France led European taste in architecture, furnishing, and the production of ornamental trifles and absurd but charming inutilities that gave a fantastically artificial atmosphere to the luxurious houses of the French nobility. English rooms were comfortably furnished; French rooms magnificently adorned. In England the Georgian furniture makers seldom allowed fashion to diminish their respect for utility, comfort, and stability; in France, seriousness and dignity in life and art gradually declined after the long reign of Louis XIV; and for over fifty years after his death in 1715 furniture design and interior decoration reflected the nature of an aristocratic society dedicated to pleasure and bored by reality.

All Europe acknowledged the supremacy of French architects and artist-craftsmen. Their leadership in the arts had been established in the last quarter of the 17th century by the vision of Colbert, Louis XIV's great minister, who mobilised creative gifts and skills as a matter of national policy; encouraged and subsidised manufacturers of porcelain, glass and tapestries, also the orna-mentalists, who made or embellished furniture: the *ébénistes*, carvers, *ciseleurs*, and *vernisseurs*. Colbert died in 1683: his policy survived for over two and a half centuries to nourish the economic strength of his country and perpetuate the French reputation for precedence in the arts.

During the latter part of Louis XIV's long reign, a new and volatile style was generated, since known as rococo and usually identified with the Louis XV period. The name did not become current until the 19th century, when it was generally applied to excessively ornate furniture and convoluted carved ornament. The word rococo was derived from *rocaille*, a term first used to describe the rock-work of the fountains and artificial grottos in the gardens of Versailles. The late R. W. Symonds suggested that it may have been coined to rhyme with the Italian word, *barocco*, and used in a derogatory sense. Rococo as an ornamental style was originated by the graceful designs of Pierre le Pautre, the engraver whose influence on style was described in Section 6. Conceived in two dimensions, rococo remained a linear art until architects, carvers, *ébénistes* and ornamentalists transposed it into three, so that asymmetrical shapes altered the form of such things as looking glass frames and girandoles, and also affected the structural anatomy of seat furniture, tables and commodes.

The rise of the rococo style coincided with fundamental changes in the general conception of furniture design; vertical lines and angles were avoided, symmetry rejected, and the severity and dignity and structural stability of the Louis XIV style were replaced by light-hearted decorative fantasies that often exhibited a wanton inconstancy. As the style matured ornament was used not only to engage and delight the eye, but to mask the facts of construction. A fresh fluidity of form characterised the new style; curves flowed into each other in unbroken continuity, conferring lightness and elegance on the sim-

A *bureau toilette* was an essential item in the furnishing of a well-appointed bedroom, for until the middle of the 18th century dressing-rooms were unknown except in very large and luxurious French houses. Like the example above, toilet and writing tables were small, compact, and graceful, with a top divided into three parts, the central division fitted with a looking glass, made to lift up and inclined backwards, sliding forward to lie flat, flush with the two sides to provide a writing surface. The sides were hinged, and when opened out could be used for toilet articles, kept in compartments below. Brushes and combs were kept in the drawer below the central division. The continuous curves introduced during the development of the rococo style gave lightness and elegance to such designs during the early part of the Louis XV period; the decorative quality was derived from the colour and marking of veneers, and inlaid roundels of ornamental woods.

Commode inlaid with floral marquetry. Gilt ormolu mounts trail interlaced scrolls across a gently curved surface and give decorative continuity to the legs and corners. This is a relatively restrained example of mid-18th century rococo.

plest articles, as exemplified by the *bureau toilette* on page 116. Continuity of line was often achieved by ignoring the properties of wood; colour and decorative quality alone were respected and displayed by *ébénistes* and chair makers; the ornamentalist dictated to such craftsmen, with the result that chests and cabinets, tables, chairs and settees seemed to be cast from some inorganic and infinitely accommodating material. Many of the motifs used in the Louis XIV style were discarded or profoundly changed, and designers riotously celebrated their emancipation from the discipline of classic ornament.

One of the influential creators of rococo was Nicholas Pineau (1684–1754), a sculptor who designed furniture and interior decoration for the French and Russian courts. He issued a series of plates, *circa* 1730, entitled *Nouveaux Desseins de Pieds de Tables et de Vases et Consoles de sculpture en bois Inventés*; and two of them illustrating console tables and brackets are reproduced on page 119. They show fecundity of invention and complete disregard for the limitations of material. Although classic ornament is almost abandoned, the proportions established by the classic orders of architecture are still in remote

Nicholas Pineau (1684–1754), a sculptor who designed furniture and interior decoration at the French and Russian courts, was one of the creators of the rococo style, and helped to establish it in France. He published a series of plates, *circa* 1730, entitled *Nouveaux Desseins de Pieds de Tables et de Vases et Consoles de sculpture en bois Inventés*, which had a considerable influence on European and English designers, and illustrated a new, adventurous independence of classic motifs, though the asymmetrical characteristics of the style had not yet appeared. The title plate and plate 5 are shown opposite. The latter was shamelessly copied by Thomas Langley. *Reproduced by courtesy of the Victoria and Albert Museum.*

Below: Marble table from plate CXLIII of *The City and Country Builder's and Workman's Treasury of Designs*, published in 1740 by Batty and Thomas Langley. The designs, which were engraved by Thomas Langley, are dated 1739, and this example, lifted from Nicholas Pineau's plate, is signed *Thos Langley Invent delin and Sculp 1739*. (Compare with the designs for frames by Chippendale and Ince and Mayhew on page 150.)

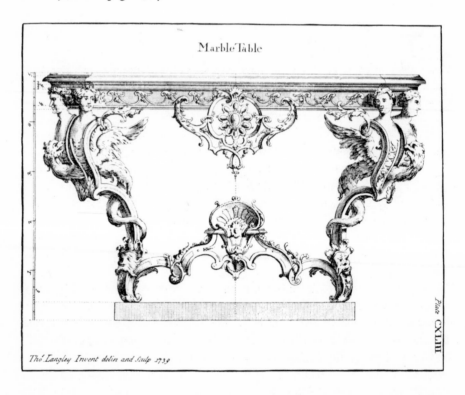

Nouveaux Desseins de Pieds de Tables et de Vases et Consoles de Sculpture en bois Inventés par le Sieur Pineau Sculpteur

a Paris chez Mariette rue S. Jacques aux colonnes d'Hercules

See caption on opposite page.

119

Veneered writing table with gilt ormolu mounts. The inlaid lines that form panels on the front and sides are related to the subdued curves of the whole design and, like the commode on page 117, assert the innate grace of the rococo style.

but effective control of composition; the universal system of design they represented was still respected as the rococo style increased in delicate complexity throughout the Louis XV period, and ultimately became attenuated and fragile. The intricate underframing of Pineau's tables and the carved supports of the brackets, recall the tortuous convolutions of 16th century strapwork, which, like early rococo was originated by draughtsmen and engravers. Some 16th and early 17th century motifs were revived, such as the cabochon; an oval, round, or egg-shaped convex ornament, framed by formalised acanthus foliations; which reappeared in a lighter and more delicate version often with a shell above, and was used on curved surfaces, like the knee of a chair or table leg. The scallop-shell, a characteristic ornament of the Louis XIV style, was transformed; the rococo shell was irregular, the edges jagged or enclosed by C-scrolls, the centre filled by foliations like those on the underframing of Pineau's console tables. The work of Pineau greatly influenced European designers. In England, Thomas Langley borrowed it without acknowledgement, and his most blatant crib, illustrated on page 118, was lifted from plate 5 of Pineau's designs, and used in *The City and Country Builder's and Workman's Treasury of Designs*, that he and his brother, Batty Langley, published in 1740.

Pineau's designs were brilliantly executed by master carvers, whose crisp rendering of intricate and profuse ornament was enhanced by gilding. The character of the style was presently enriched by an increasing use of gilt bronze mounts, and the skill of the *ciseleur* gave fresh emphasis to asymmetrical ornament, as exemplified by the commode on page 117 and the bow-fronted corner cupboard shown below. Decorative woods were used extensively; native fruit woods like cherry and plum; mahogany was imported, also exotic timbers such as purpleheart, sandalwood, jacaranda and coralwood; in the latter part of the Louis XV period, rosewood supplied a range of glowing, russet hues. The commode on page 117 is inlaid with floral marquetry, and woods of many colours were employed by inlayers for rococo compositions: bouquets and baskets of flowers, sprays of leaves,

Left: A small secrétaire with the writing space open, showing the three shallow drawers and shelf space within. Veneered in ornamental woods and enriched with ormolu mounts. Mid-18th century. *Right*: Corner cupboard of the same date. The elongated curves of the bronze mounts, the acanthus scrolls, Bacchante mask above and spray of roses below, frame a panel decorated with a formalised Chinese landscape. *The cupboard is in the Wallace Collection.*

Interior of salon, Hotel Cours D'Albert à Bordeaux. Continuous curves characterise the treatment of walls and fireplace and a feathery delicacy gives the decoration an air of fragility. Compare this example of early Louis XV rococo with the interior opposite.

wreaths, ribbons, trophies of musical instruments in place of the martial trophies of the previous reign, and groups of figures, variously engaged in conversation, dancing or dalliance. Some plain articles of furniture, in beech, birch or other common woods, were dipped in dye, usually of a reddish tint, and subsequently polished. Furniture was frequently painted to match the background colour of a panelled room or to harmonise with the curtains and upholstery.

The taste for Chinese and Japanese lacquer that gained extensive popularity during the last two decades of Louis XIV's reign, had been satisfied by imports from the Far East that came mainly through Holland. Lacquered panels were framed in the doors of cabinets and other types of case furniture, although they were originally designed for totally different uses; but when the ecstatic curves of emergent rococo changed the shape of furniture, cabinet-makers were unable to insert the flat panels imported from China; so they followed the example of Dutch makers, and shipped drawer-fronts and door panels to China, "in the white", to use a trade term, where they were decorated by oriental artists and returned for use after an interval of several months. These lacquers were usually black or very deep brown, and occasionally red, with gold reliefs. From the late 17th century to the death of Louis XIV French *vernisseurs* attempted to imitate them; but although they never succeeded in producing lacquer of a comparable quality, by 1730 the French industry was so accomplished that it was able to compete with that of the Far East, and was

Salle à manger archevêché de Bordeaux. Before the end of the Louis XV period classic motifs had reappeared and moulded detail became bolder. No phase of rococo was robust, but extreme delicacy and fragility had lost their appeal before the style became outmoded.

123

far in advance of Dutch and English lacquer. Developing concurrently with the rococo style, French lacquer extended the taste for Chinese decoration; the rustic landscapes, diversified with figures as stylised as those from a pack of cards; the strangely-shaped trees, unfamiliar birds and blossoms, and Celestial architecture, so different from anything European, exerted an almost magical appeal, and became an integral part of the modish environment in France. An affinity between rococo ornament and Chinese art was acknowledged and exploited, although what passed for Chinese art in Europe was as remote from the reality as European ideas about the character of contemporary Chinese civilisation.

The supremacy of French lacquer owed much to the Martin family of artist-craftsmen, who invented, perfected and patented a particularly brilliant translucent lacquer that became known by the generic name of *Vernis Martin*. The family consisted of four brothers: Guillaume, Simon Étienne, Julien and Robert, of whom the most outstanding was Robert (1706–65). By the mid-18th century the Brothers Martin were directing at least three lacquer-producing factories in Paris that were classed in 1748 as a "manufacture nationale". Robert enjoyed the patronage of La Pompadour; and his son, Jean Alexandre Martin, was appointed *vernisseur du Roy* at the court of Frederick the Great. Lacquers by the famous brothers were identified with polished luxury.

Bronze mounts, mentioned earlier, ceased to be mere decorative adjuncts to the more elaborate commodes, tables and bureaux; they dominated design to such an extent that materials used in construction were subordinated to the effective display of such superb examples of the *ciseleur's* art; after casting they were refined by the chaser and the burin, and gilded with *or moulu*, ground gold, a term used in France during and after the 16th century to describe gold leaf for gilding metals and in England, since the late 18th century, for articles of gilt bronze or brass as well as gilt mounts. The commode on page 117, and the corner cupboard on page 121, show the decorative dominance of ormolu; so do the handles and escutcheons, the mounts on the angles and casings on the feet of the veneered writing table on page 120. Slender fillets of metal often protected the angles of veneered furniture.

Various durable and decorative materials were used for the tops of consoles and commodes, chiefly in white or coloured marble, and for small and delicate pieces of furniture, alabaster, onyx, mosaics of precious stones and, towards the end of the period, china; medallions of that fragile and fashionable material were also inlaid in mahogany panels. A circular plaque of

124

Beds were still dominated by curtains depending from a canopy, though in this mid-18th century example the canopy has become vestigial and the curtains purely decorative. The exposed wooden frame of such a bed would be gilded or painted to match the interior decoration of the bedroom.

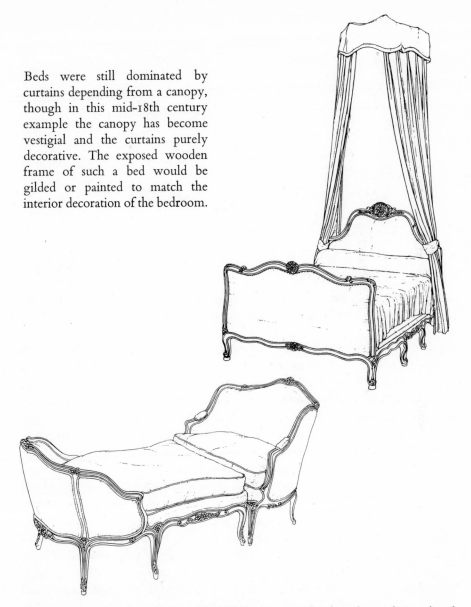

A duchesse, consisting of a low-backed long seat and a broad armchair, placed together to form a day-bed. Some examples consisted of two tub-backed easy chairs with a stool between them: such composite chairs and stools were introduced to England after the mid-18th century. (See page 196.)

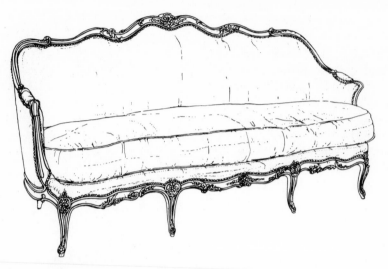

Settee with carved and moulded frame of polished wood, the junction of frame and fabric marked by lines of dome-headed gilt nails. *Circa* 1750.

apple-green Sèvres porcelain, painted with exotic birds perched on a tree, is set in the top of a guéridon-table, in the Wallace Collection. The guéridon or guéridon-table, had evolved from a small stand that supported some form of light such as a candelabrum; it was introduced in France in the mid-17th century, originally in the form of a Negro figure holding a tray or a light. The name may have been taken from an African whose death is mourned in a song that was popular in France in the early 17th century, and it has been suggested that Guéridon was a character in a ballet who in one scene held up a torch while a circle of girls danced round him. But the guéridon-table of the mid- and late-18th century was transformed; its original function as a lamp support was forgotten; and it became an ornamental but useful occasional table, often with shelves below and a cupboard under the top. (See page 187.) Like the dumb waiter, that French cabinet-makers invented, it was a compact, decorative, and convenient article. The dumb waiter was one of many inventions that added to the graces of life: writing tables, toilet and jewel tables, and work-tables or *chiffonnieres*, exquisitely made, furnished the bed-rooms and boudoirs where excellence of workmanship celebrated the supremacy of luxury. No furniture before or since has attained such perfection of finish or exhibited such triviality of purpose.

The rococo style has been wrongly associated with the name of La Pompadour: it was on the wane before she was established at Versailles as "maitresse en tître", in 1745, and her personal preference was for simple and even severe designs. Her impeccable taste is apparent in the tranquil beauty of the Petit Trianon, designed for her by Ange Jacques Gabriel. She encouraged the development of the Neo-classical style that followed rococo and captivated French society early in the 1760s. Everything had to be à la Grecque: the baubles and trinkets worn or carried by men and women of fashion: the ornaments that thronged the shelves of cabinets and brackets, the ormolu mounts on furniture, and finally the shape of case and seat furniture, displayed an elegant orderliness, vastly different from the frolics of rococo. After the death of La Pompadour in 1764, the transient dignity and restraint of early Neo-classic was lost; curvilinear shapes reappeared, and though asymmetrical composition was discarded, the new fashions in furniture design were as engaging, fantastic and remote from sober realism as anything rococo. No other style, dedicated to ostentation, has commanded such superlative skill or illustrated the unconscious preparations of an aristocracy for class-suicide.

Two mid-18th century chairs. *Left:* Single chair with caned back and seat and boldly carved frame. *Right:* Armchair with caned back and sides and padded arms: curves alone supply the decorative character.

127

SECTION 9. RESURGENCE OF ENGLISH BAROQUE

The Georgian age that began with the accession of George I and ended when George IV died in 1830 has been sub-divided, so we have Early Georgian, 1714 to about 1735; mid-Georgian, including the 1740s and '50s; and late Georgian, a term applicable to the last seventy years of the period though seldom used, because the names of the various styles, movements in taste and romantic revivals which occurred during that time are more memorably descriptive. The harmonies of the Queen Anne style were followed by a resurgence of Baroque, just as lively and gay as the Carolean version, though less exuberant; form was never overwhelmed by a carapace of carved ornament, as on the silvered pinewood stand of the japanned cabinet on page 83; furniture was decorated and mouldings enriched with delicate precision, and the technique of carving was improved by the increased use of gesso, which allowed work in low relief to be executed with a new freedom, unrestricted by the limitations imposed by the grain of wood. Gesso, a composition of parchment size and whitening built up in successive layers on a wood ground, was known to mediaeval craftsmen, and had been reintroduced to England from Italy in the second half of the 17th century. Although it had been used occasionally since Charles II's reign, gesso carved into soft and flowing lines and gilded became a characteristic of the new phase of Baroque in the early Georgian period.

That period began in the shadow of Teutonic taste, which was favoured by George I; some of the luxurious furniture made under Court influence was decidedly overweight; but the skill of English makers and the genius of designers such as William Kent and his contemporaries restrained overt obesity; the graces of the Queen Anne style were never lost, they were amplified, while fresh and discerning studies of antique examples brought a new, florid vitality to ornament. William Kent (?1685–1748) interpreted Baroque in his own vehement manner, and as Horace Walpole recorded later, "his oracle was so much consulted by all who affected taste, that nothing was thought complete without his assistance. He was not only consulted for furniture, as frames of pictures, glasses, tables, chairs, &c, but for plate, for a barge, for a cradle". The control of the architect as the master-designer, responsible

128

Carved and gilt side table, with scrolls, swags and grotesque mask. The scrolled upper parts of the legs are ornamented with lightly carved fish scales, a form of decoration used on the chairs on page 132. Reproduced from *Some Designs of Mr. Inigo Jones and Mr. Wm. Kent*, published by John Vardy, 1744.

for every branch of design, was already established. Nearly all Kent's tables, cabinets, bookcases and seat furniture were conceived as parts of an architectural composition; and were lavishly decorated with carved and gilt acanthus scrolls, variations of the Greek key pattern, shells, and vividly realistic masks, grotesque faces or ferocious lions. These masks appeared on the knees of cabriole legs, on the arms and backs of chairs and settees, on the aprons of tables and cabinet stands. Chair and table legs terminated in claw-and-ball feet, or were carved to represent a shaggy paw or a hoof.

Mahogany now provided carvers with a rewarding material. The wood, known in the late 17th century, was grown in Jamaica, and as that island long remained the chief source of supply it was called Jamaica wood when it came into use for furniture in the third and fourth decades of the 18th century, though as a material it had no marked effect on design until the mid-Georgian period when it was used extensively by Thomas Chippendale and his contemporaries. Jamaican merchants in addition to dealing in timber grown in the island, imported Spanish mahogany from Cuba and Honduras and shipped it to England. Varieties of the wood were used consistently until the close of the 19th century.

Carved console table, gesso on wood, gilt. Like the side tables opposite the design is in the style of William Kent. The eagle device, used as a support, was introduced in the early 18th century.

Side table with carved and scrolled legs. The scrolls, florid carving and general design are comparable with the table by Kent on page 129.
Both examples in the Victoria and Albert Museum.

Above: Carved side table in mahogany, with gilt enrichments. The lower parts of the legs are fluted and terminate in paw feet. *Circa* 1730–35. The influence of Kent is apparent in the design. *Below:* Walnut side table with marble top. The carved ornament is slightly influenced by the rococo style, which is revealed by the C-scrolls on the inner side of the legs and the coquillage in the centre of the apron. The legs end in talon-and-ball feet.

Both examples in the Victoria and Albert Museum.

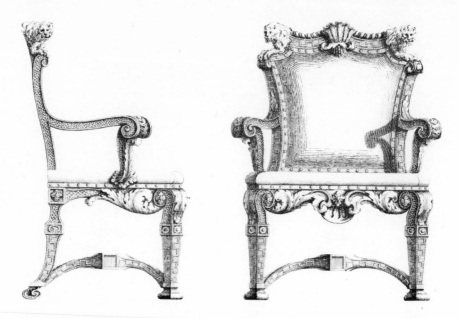

Carved and gilt armchair with lion terminals on the top rail, and scrolls on the arms and upper part of front legs. Compare with the Kent table on page 129. Reproduced from *Some Designs of Mr. Inigo Jones and Mr. Wm. Kent*, published by John Vardy, 1744.

The early Georgian period is distinguished by a mastery of the principles of architectural composition, which encouraged a closer association between the form and function of furniture, and such interior features as windows and the piers between them. The pier glass and the pier table had been introduced in the late 17th century, and during the 1720s and '30s such articles were often designed as a single decorative unit. Knowledge of architectural composition was so widely diffused that even a village joiner, making occasional pieces of case furniture for the local squire—a cupboard, a bookcase, a blanket chest or a clothes press—could not be faulted in proportions or moulded detail. He had copy books to guide him, with plates on the classic orders, some written with the authority and knowledge of a great architect like James Gibbs (1682–1754), who published *A Book of Architecture* in 1728, containing many of his own designs, and six years later his *Rules for Drawing the Several Parts of Architecture*. During the second quarter of the century such works occasionally illustrated a few suggestions for furniture, sometimes by an architect like William Jones, who issued in 1739 a collection of copper-plate engravings in book form entitled: *The Gentlemens or Builders Companion, Containing Variety of usefull Designs for Doors, Gateways, Peers, Pavilions, Temples, Chimney-*

pieces, Slab Tables, Pier Glasses, or Tabernacle Frames, Ceiling Pieces, &c. He included designs for looking glass frames, marble-topped tables, and some indifferent chimneypieces. Far more varied and prolific guidance for builders, joiners and cabinet-makers was provided by Batty Langley (1696–1751) who, with his brother Thomas, an engraver, established a school of architectural drawing in Soho about 1740. As mentioned in the previous section, Thomas Langley blatantly lifted designs from French sources (German as well): the best known work of the brothers, issued in 1740, was *The City and Country Builder's and Workman's Treasury of Designs*. The plates included some monumental examples of case furniture, architecturally correct in detail and proportions, but conceived without knowledge of or sympathy with wood as a material: they might indeed have been intended for execution in stone. The

Left: One of a set of chairs in mahogany designed by William Kent, with upholstered seat and back, trimmed with brass-headed nails. The seat rail is ornamented with a wave device, and the legs with their lightly carved knees, end in knurl feet. *Reproduced by permission of the late R. W. Symonds. Right*: Single chair in mahogany with shaped seat. The lion masks carved on the knees rise into the seat rail. *Circa* 1730. There is a comparable example in the Victoria and Albert Museum, on loan from the Leicester Museum and Art Gallery.

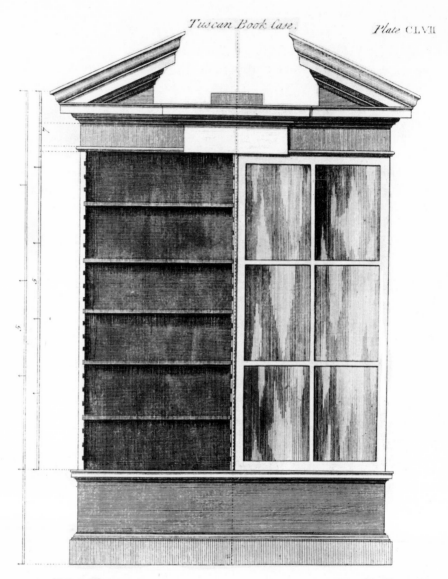

Batty Langley Invent 1730.   *Thos Langley Sculp.*

Architectural bookcase, designed by Batty Langley, which he described as Tuscan. Like many of Langley's monumental designs for case furniture, this seems to be intended for execution in stone rather than wood. Reproduced on a slightly smaller scale from plate CLVII of *The City and Country Builder's and Workman's Treasury of Designs.* (London: 1739.)

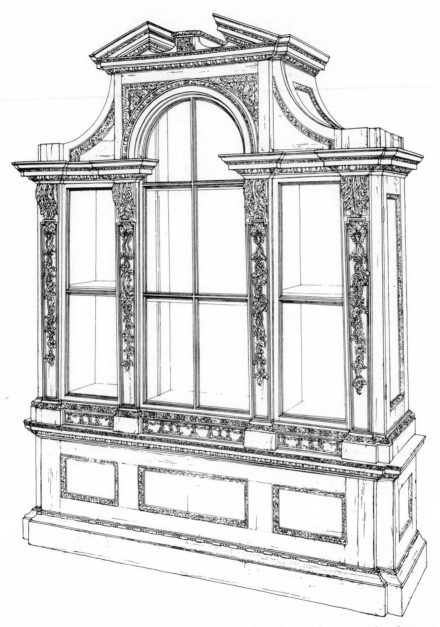

Pinewood bookcase, carved and painted, with gilt enrichments. The design is marked by the influence of William Kent. *Circa* 1730. *In the Victoria and Albert Museum.*

Left: Early Georgian looking glass frame in mahogany with carved ornament and gilt enrichment. *Formerly in the collection of the late Robert Atkinson, F.R.I.B.A. Right*: Pinewood frame with burr walnut veneer and gilt gesso ornament. *Circa 1730. In the Victoria and Albert Museum.* Both examples are surmounted by swan-neck broken pediments.

influence of such uninspired mentors might have had an unfortunate effect on furniture design, but men at the bench were competent to correct the errors of mere draughtsmen. Compare the so-called "Tuscan" bookcase on page 134 with the design by William Kent that faces it: both are architectural bookcases, but the contrast between the work of a master-designer and that of a hack draughtsman is marked, even though Batty Langley played for safety by keeping his bookcase plain, and using sash doors, as they were termed in the mid-18th century.

The Early Georgian style, that owed so much to William Kent, was a lusty, energetic style; by the second quarter of the century it had shed all suggestion of placid immobility, inherited from German ideas. Kent, happily immune from Teutonic taste, was certainly influenced by French ideas, especially by the engravings of Jean Bérain, and his handling of antique ornament was original and masterly. Like the great designers who came after him, Kent knew where to place ornament, never lost control of it, and conferred on all his designs the impeccable proportions of classic architecture.

SECTION 10. CHIPPENDALE AND MID-GEORGIAN STYLE

Because he published a lavishly illustrated trade catalogue, Thomas Chippendale's name has become associated with much of the robust, well-proportioned case and seat furniture made during the mid-18th century; he was the first cabinet-maker to issue a book of designs, which appeared in 1754 and was called *The Gentleman and Cabinet Maker's Director*. A second edition with the same contents was published in 1755 and a third, with additional plates, in 1762. Thomas Chippendale, the elder, who was baptised at Otley Parish Church, Yorkshire, June 5th, 1718, established a business in London, although it is not known when he settled there; in 1749 he was living in Conduit Court, Long Acre; in 1752 at Somerset or Northumberland Court in the Strand; and in 1753 or 1754 he moved to 60 St. Martin's Lane. After his death in 1779 the business was carried on there by his eldest son, Thomas (1749–1822). The *Director* was a catalogue of Chippendale's wares, and a most influential copy book. In the preface the author said: "Upon the whole I have given no design but what may be executed with advantage by the hands of a skilled workman, tho' some of the profession have been diligent enough to represent them (especially those after the Gothic and Chinese manner) as so many specious drawings impossible to be worked off by any mechanic whatsoever. I will not scruple to attribute this to malice, ignorance and inability: And I am confident I can convince all Noblemen, Gentlemen, or others, who will honour me with their commands, that every design in the book can be improved, both as to beauty and enrichment in the execution of it, by their most obedient servant, Thomas Chippendale."

At the time the plates were being engraved for the *Director* by Matthias Lock and Henry Copland, two designers and ornamentalists, whom Chippendale employed, furniture design was no longer in a period of transition: the bold curves and copious ornament of the Early Georgian style were replaced by more austere conceptions of shape, that developed side by side with the insinuating gaiety of rococo. Chippendale and his contemporaries worked in a style that could be interpreted by country makers as well as practised by

137

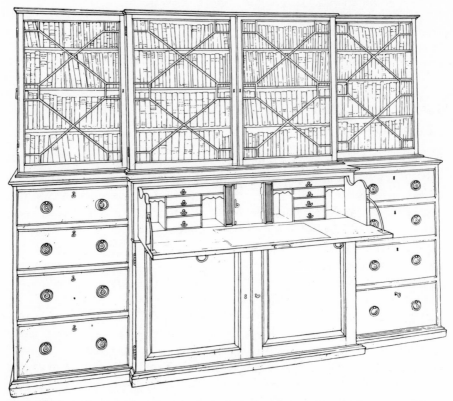

Large library bookcase, with escritoire, the writing space lowered on a quadrant. There are cupboards below, and a double bank of drawers. The glazing bars of the bookcase are slender and flat in section. This is a plain, straightforward piece of cabinet-makers' work, well-proportioned but without the architectural character of the bookcase and press shown opposite. Mahogany. *Circa* 1760–70. *Formerly in the possession of Miss Muriel Barron.*

Pedestal writing table of carved mahogany, dated 1751. The angles at the front have fluted colonettes; the arched knee-hole is flanked by fluted and reeded Ionic pilasters rising from moulded and facetted plinths. The table rests on cabriole bracket feet. *In the Victoria and Albert Museum.*

Left: Mahogany bookcase with sash-doors, fall front escritoire drawer, shallow knee-hole with cupboard behind, flanked by two large cupboards. *Circa* 1740–50. *Right*: Cedar-lined mahogany press with drawers below. Like the pedestal writing table opposite this shows the influence of architects on furniture design, particularly in the swan-neck pediment, the fluted Doric pilasters with triglyphs above, the moulding and detail of the cornice, and the fluted colonettes rising from plinths at the front angles of the lower part. The press rests on cabriole bracket feet. *Circa* 1745–50. *Both examples formerly in the collection of the late Robert Atkinson, F.R.I.B.A.*

Left: Mahogany tallboy resting on pierced bracket feet. *Right*: Mahogany chest on stand, supported on turned legs with club feet. Both examples are ornamented by a blind fret on the frieze; both date from the mid-18th century.

such fashionable firms as Vile and Cobb; a style that was architectural without being monumental, that followed classic proportions and borrowed classic detail, a debt Chippendale acknowledged in the opening sentences of his preface. "Of all the Arts which are either improved or ornamented by Architecture," he said, "that of CABINET-MAKING is not only the most useful and ornamental, but capable of receiving as great Assistance from it as any whatever. I have therefore prefixed to the following Designs a Short Explanation of the Five Orders. Without an Acquaintance with this Science, and some Knowledge of the Rules of Perspective, the Cabinet-Maker cannot make the Designs of his Work intelligible, nor shew, in a little Compass, the whole Conduct and Effect of the Piece. These, therefore, ought to be carefully studied by every one who would excel in this Branch, since they are the very Soul and Basis of his Art."

The first eight plates of the *Director* were occupied by the Tuscan, Doric, Ionic, Corinthian and Composite orders, with their various details. Columns and pilasters were adapted and used on case furniture; the examples on pages 138 and 139 show how such features were incorporated in the design; they were not merely applied; they were part of a dextrous composition in wood. Both suggest the influence of architects' taste; both suggest that their makers enjoyed a close and discerning knowledge of the orders. They represent the outstanding characteristics of the classic, mid-Georgian style, emphatically national, immune from the contemporary invasion of foreign taste, unmarked by the freaks and fantasies of exotic and antiquarian fashions. Benefits derived from the curvilinear revolution were not lost; the cabriole leg was still used, though with less frequency, and the square-sectioned straight leg was introduced, sometimes tapering towards the foot. The claw-and-ball foot was retained, also the club foot with a pad or base, and the knurl foot and the up-

Below: Breakfast table in mahogany, with open fret doors and sides to the cupboard below the top and two hinged drop leaves. This is similar to the design on plate LIII of Chippendale's *Director*, third edition (1762). *Right:* Dumb waiter in mahogany.

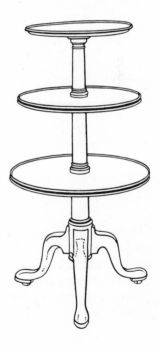

141

turned whorl foot, with their tight, volute-like scrolls were frequently used. Naturalistic forms became popular; the club foot was developed as a stylised hoof, and many chairmakers used the cloven hoof as a leg terminal. Some of Chippendale's designs for chairs and tables had legs resting on guttae feet, copied from the small drop-like ornaments above and below the triglyphs of the Doric frieze. Chests and book cases were often supported on bracket feet, which were sometimes ornamented with pierced frets like those on the mahogany tallboy on page 140, or, when cabriole brackets were used, the knees were adorned with carved gadrooning. English makers between 1730 and 1760 gave an air of tranquil stability to case furniture, especially to large architectural bookcases with their broken pediments and accurately detailed

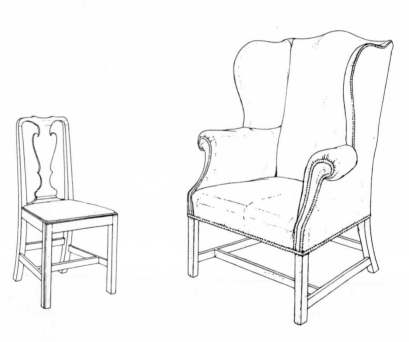

Above, left: The characteristic splat of early 18th century chairs survived, and in this single chair a Queen Anne back is associated with the square-sectioned legs of the middle years. *Above, right:* The form of the winged easy chair was established by the late 17th century, and this example, *circa* 1750–60, is a much simplified version of the elegant upholstered armchair on page 111. *Both chairs in the possession of Mrs Frances Custance.*

LANDALL & GORDON.

Joyners, Cabinet, & Chair - Makers
At ye Griffin & Chair in Little Argyle Street
by Swallow Street.
Makes all sorts of Tables, Chairs, Setee-Beds,
Looking-Glasses, Picture-frames, Window-
Blinds, & all sorts of Cabinet Work

The trade card of Landall and Gordon, in business *circa* 1750. The chair suggests the early Georgian style, but a contemporary fashion is acknowledged by the rococo C-scrolls that support the griffin. *Reproduced by courtesy of the Trustees of the British Museum.*

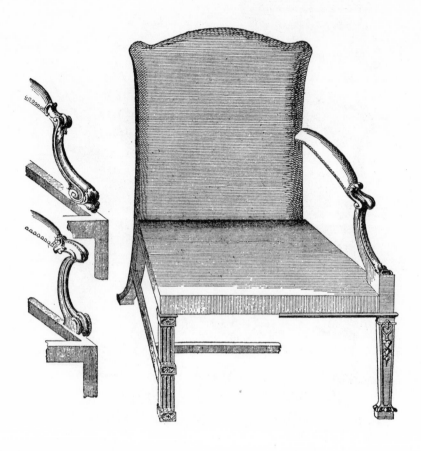

Chippendale's design for an armchair, reproduced from plate XIX of the *Director*, third edition (1762). Such open-sided types were known in the mid-18th century as "French chairs", and the arms and legs were shaped and ornamented in a variety of ways: this example shows three forms of arm, one of them, below on the left, clearly descended from the earlier scroll-over type. Seat and back are continuous, and are stuffed and covered with Spanish leather or damask. Brass headed nails are used only on the upholstered arm pads. One of the alternative suggestions for front legs is tapered: both are of square section. The top of the back reproduces the same line, with upturned corners, as the chair shown opposite, below left: a characteristic of Chippendale's chair backs. (See Ribbon back chair top left, page 156.)

mouldings: the rather heavy glazing bars of the sash bookcase were replaced by thinner moulded or often flat-sectioned bars, arranged in geometric patterns as on the large library case, *circa* 1760–70, on page 138.

The range and variety of furniture available in the period is suggested by an advertisement that appeared in *The Whitehall Evening-Post; or, London Intelligencer*, for June 26–28, 1760, which read as follows:—

"This Day was publish'd, in One Neat Volume, Octavo, (price 6s. sew'd, bound 7s) HOUSEHOLD FURNITURE in genteel Taste, for the Year 1760. By a Society of Upholsterers, Cabinet-Makers, &c. Containing upwards of One Hundred and Eighty Designs on Sixty Copper-plates. Beautifully Engraved by M. Darly. Consisting of China, Breakfast, Side-Board, Dressing, Toilet, Card, Writing, Claw, Library, Slab, and Night Tables; Chairs, Couches, French Stools, Cabinets, Commodes, China Shelves and Cases, Trays, Chests, Stands for Candles, Tea Kettles, Pedestals, Stair-Case Lights, Bureaus, Beds, Ornamental Bed-Posts, Corniches, Brackets, Fire-Screens, Desk, Book and Clock-Cases, Frames for Glasses, Sconce and Chimney-Pieces, Girandoles, Lanthorns, Chandalears, &c &c with Scales. Printed for Robert Sayer, Map and Printseller, at the Golden Buck in Fleet-Street."

Mathias Darly, mentioned in that advertisement, was an engraver and publisher, who had produced, in 1750–51, a work called *A New Book of*

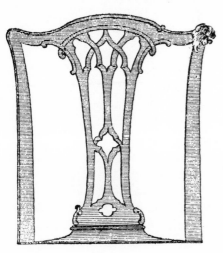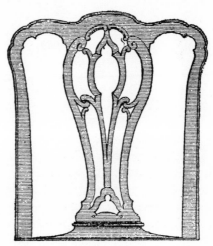

Two designs for chair backs, reproduced from plate XVI of Chippendale's *Director*, third edition (1762).

Posted bed with spiral turning and fluting on the front columns. *Circa* 1750–60. *In the possession of John Atkinson, Esq., F.R.I.B.A.*

Chinese, Gothic and Modern Chairs, an indifferent performance that did little for his reputation as a designer; but he was an accomplished engraver, and was employed by Chippendale for some of the plates in the *Director*, and all but the last six plates in *The Universal System of Household Furniture*, by Ince and Mayhew, bear his signature. The bold, masculine outline of chairs in the *Director* are wholly different in character from Darly's feeble designs. The illustrations on pages 144 and 157, show the strength and comfort of Chippendale's seat furniture. The mid-Georgian style could accommodate the vagaries of the Rococo, Chinese and Gothic taste, described in the next two sections, not only in seats, but in tables, beds and every form of case furniture.

SECTION 11. ENGLISH ROCOCO AND THE CHINESE TASTE

The rococo style that reached maturity in France during the third decade of the 18th century, crossed to England late in the 1730s where it succeeded the florid, almost boisterous baroque of William Kent. The affinity between rococo and Chinese art was in its favour, for the Chinese Taste was attracting the interest of the modish, and while a purely French ornamental style might have been excluded as freakish and unstable, the semi-oriental character of rococo was immediately acceptable. Not that French fashions were unpopular; far from it; their popularity was remarked and criticised by William Whitehead who said what he thought about them, all unsweetened, in *The World*. "There is a folly indeed (for I will not call it a vice) with which the ladies of this age are particularly charged," he wrote; "it is, that not only their airs and their dress, but even their faces are French. I wish with all my heart that I could preserve my integrity, and vindicate my fair country-women from this imputation; but I am sorry to say it, what by travelling abroad, and by French milliners, mantua-makers and hair-dressers at home, our politest assemblies seem to be filled with foreigners." (Letter 75, June 6th, 1754.)

The "politest assemblies" flirted and gossiped against a background that attested the potency of French taste. Fashionable ladies and gentlemen in dazzling, exquisite clothes moved from group to group, their smiles and gestures reflected by tall looking-glasses, enclosed by carved and gilded frames; and those frames and the chandeliers and girandoles from which wax candles sprouted, and the side tables and seat furniture, all exhibited a decorative opulence, light and gay and wholly different in character from the bold curves and tumescent ornament of the early Georgian period. Rococo was tamed and anglicised by Thomas Chippendale and his contemporaries. The first English interpreters of the style were silversmiths and engravers, who introduced asymmetrical ornament on the shields that framed coats of arms engraved on silver plate, and enlivened the chapter-headings of books, the borders of book plates, tradesmen's cards and billheads, with C-scrolls, exiguous acanthus foliations, stalactites, birds and flowers. These preliminary, two-dimensional flirtations with rococo soon became a serious affair when

Frontispiece from *Fables for the Female Sex*, published in London, 1744. The ornate looking glass frame and the marble slab with dolphin supports are typical of an engraver's conception of rococo ornament. (See opposite page.)

Rococo device from the title page of *Fables for the Female Sex*, a rather muddled composition, with conflicting elements, but again exemplifying the engraver's interpretation of the rococo style. (See opposite page.)

furniture-makers, especially carvers, discovered the liberties they could take with familiar classical motifs.

Since the time of Charles II, the carver and gilder had united their skills, and established a significant and independent trade of their own, interpreting the work of fashionable designers, and contributing their own creative ideas to the shape and decoration of furniture. In the development of English rococo, their influence established the preference for crisply carved wood ornament instead of the ormolu mounts devised by French *ciseleurs*, and as the most active exponents of the style in the mid-18th century, they endowed it with a distinctive national character, though much of their work, as well as that of cabinet-makers and upholsterers, was commercially described as being "in the French taste". The initial inspiration certainly came from France, but there was a fundamental difference between French and English rococo; the difference between nerves and muscles. The conceptions of French ornamentalists frequently suggested a febrile, almost hysterical fidgetiness; those of English carvers, a lithe agility, for they generally used a soft wood, such as pine, that allowed sharply defined renderings of sinuous

effectinely effectively

Above: Frame for a marble slab: Chippendale's nearest approach to structural distortion. From plate CLXXV of the *Director* (third edition, 1762). *Below:* A far more extravagant and fragile design, by Ince and Mayhew, reproduced from plate LXXIV of *The Universal System of Household Furniture.*

ornamental forms. Joints and faults in the wood were smoothed over with gesso; surfaces were gilt, some burnished, some matt, a contrast that gave lambent richness to carved work, which was lost when a dark, polished wood like mahogany was used. Without gold, rococo parted with its piquancy. Some French furniture in the later phases of the style was webbed over with frothy shreds of ornament that blurred or obliterated or even deformed structural lines; that seldom happened in England.

Mathias Lock, Henry Copland, and that master-carver, Thomas Johnson gave generous substance to English rococo. Cabinet-makers rejected the bulging, three-dimensional curves of carcase furniture used by French designers; their concessions to such ornamental shapes stopped short at a serpentine or a bowed front to a commode or a press. Nothing comparable with French distortion of chair or table frames was allowed. Chippendale's nearest approach to structural distortion is illustrated by the frame for a marble slab, reproduced opposite from plate CLXXV of the *Director*. Nothing that impaired comfort or condoned fragility would have been acceptable to English patrons, who might be, and often were, whimsical, eccentric and exacting, but were immune from the enslavement to fatuous fashions that ultimately debased French rococo. Like the frame just mentioned, Chippen-

Right: Pole screen supported on rococo stand. Reproduced on a smaller scale from Chippendale's *Director* (third edition, 1762), plate CLVI. *Below:* Two claw tables on rococo stands, reproduced on a smaller scale from *Genteel Household Furniture in the Present Taste.* (Second edition, undated, but probably issued in 1765. The first edition was dated 1760.)

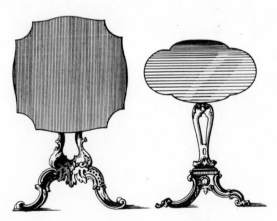

151

Two girandoles from Chippendale's
Director (third edition, 1762). They
appear, with those shown on the
opposite page, on plate CLXXVII.
The design above includes a classic
ruin, an Ionic column and two
arches; the example on the left also
has an architectural ruin: both are
surrounded by scrolls and foliage.

Three girandoles completing the group of five on plate CLXXVII of the *Director*. (See opposite page.) Architectural fragments appear in two of the examples, Gothic in character, but so subdued by competing rococo motifs that they could hardly be described as "in the Gothic taste".

Chippendale's designs for rococo chimneypieces are shown here and opposite. Both are reproduced, on a smaller scale, from plate CLXXXI of the *Director* (third edition, 1762).

dale's "Ribband-back" chairs were an exception. Three alternative designs, from the first edition of the *Director* (1754), are shown on page 156. The splats, carved to simulate interlaced ribbons, were too delicate; not even the finest mahogany could resist strain when carved into wafer-thin convolutions, with the grain of the wood running in all directions. Chippendale claimed that "Several sets have been made, which have given entire Satisfaction". But very few were actually made, and seldom if ever by provincial makers.

Chippendale's control of rococo ornament is exemplified by his designs for chimneypieces, reproduced opposite and above from plate CLXXXI of the

Alternative design for a rococo chimneypiece from Chippendale's *Director*. (See opposite page.) In both examples different treatments are given for the sides of fireplaces and chimney glasses.

Director, which show alternative treatments for the mantelpieces and the chimney glasses, and various motifs are associated without conflict or confusion. English rococo was short-lived; far less ornate in execution than the examples engraved on the plates published by Chippendale, Lock, Copland, or Ince and Mayhew, which tended to revert to the original linear conception of the style; but the prodigal flourishes and complexities conceived on a drawing board and minutely executed by engravers, were subdued by the discipline of a third dimension, and by the skill and abundant common sense of English craftsmen. Thomas Johnson was the carver who gave English

Continued on page 160

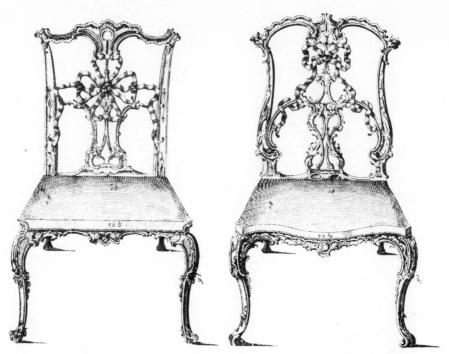

Above and right: Three "Ribband
Back" chairs, from Chippendale's
Director (first edition, 1754). Although Chippendale asserted that
"Several sets have been made, which
have given entire Satisfaction," very
few of these fragile rococo designs
were executed.

Above, left: Armchair in mahogany carved with rococo ornament, based on Chippendale's design, *below*, on plate XXII of the *Director* (third edition, 1762).

Left: Armchair in the "French Taste," which shows how competently English makers used rococo ornament, and conveyed the characteristics of the style without surrendering basic stability. The chairs on this page avoid the excessive curvature of the legs characteristic of contemporary French chairs and settees, which often suggested that they might yield to the weight of those seated on them, and, when released from it, would resume their normal shape. English makers avoided the appearance of such elastic fragility.

157

Sofa with rococo ornament carved on the frame. Reproduced on a smaller scale from plate XXX of Chippendale's *Director* (third edition, 1762).

French corner chair or short settee, reproduced from plate LVII of *The Universal System of Household Furniture*, by Ince and Mayhew (London: 1759–62).

Two French stools, described as "Designs for stools for recesses of Windows," reproduced from plate LXI of *The Universal System of Household Furniture*, by Ince and Mayhew. On the lower example alternative designs are shown for the legs. (See French corner chair opposite.)

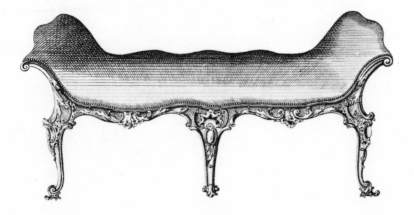

rococo its most cogent and mature form. His work was robust, vigorous, and never finical. Fluidity of line and subtlety of composition differentiate his designs from those of Chippendale or Ince and Mayhew; and those qualities are apparent in the plates of his first book, *Twelve Girandoles*, published in 1755. Girandoles were then equated with luxury and opulence, and those designed by Johnson illustrate his ability to unite formalised rococo with boldly naturalistic motifs. In 1758 he published his second work, *The Book of the Carver*, with 53 engraved plates; and between 1756 and 1758 he issued, in monthly parts, *One Hundred and Fifty New Designs*. He influenced the ideas of Ince and Mayhew, who began to publish in 1759 *The Universal System of Household Furniture*, which contained over 300 designs, and was completed in 1762, when it appeared in book form, though it is undated. The title page and notes on the plates were printed in French and English, and the authors obviously expected their book to circulate in France as books and plates of French designs circulated in England.

The Chinese taste, that had reached England in the mid-17th century, did not expand into a fashion until after the Restoration, and for over seventy years its manifestations were confined to surface decoration, apart from one revolutionary exception, introduced during the first decade of the 18th

"Toylet table," reproduced on a smaller scale from Chippendale's *Director* (third edition, 1762), plate CXIX. Draperies completely conceal any framework, and such articles resembled the sculptural effect of fabric-covered furniture of the late 17th and early 18th centuries.

Couch bed with ornate rococo canopy, designed by Chippendale and reproduced from plate L of the *Director* (third edition, 1762). Like the beds of the late 17th century, this is an upholsterer's fantasy, and the canopy is a rococo extravaganza. Compare with Marot's design on page 99.

century, namely the bended-back chair, with a splat curved to accommodate human contours and a top rail shaped like a milkmaid's yoke. In 1953 the late R. W. Symonds identified a Chinese prototype, for similar chairs had been imported from China by the East India Company, and adapted by English makers. No other change in the form of furniture was attributable to Chinese influence during the first third of the 18th century, but thereafter ornamental devices familiar in Chinese decoration were detached from their context and frequently associated with the rococo motifs. Of these, the pagoda with its pendant bells, pointed finials and upturned eaves, was elegantly varied, often incorporated in an intricate geometric fret, or used independently as a terminal device on case furniture, or a surmount on the frame of a looking glass, or the yoke rail of a chair or settee back. The widespread adoption of such motifs transformed the character of the Chinese taste; a polite and informed interest in *chinoiserie*, hitherto restricted to collecting porcelain, embroideries, painted silks, oriental lacquered cabinets and screens, was now extended to the interior decoration and furnishing of complete rooms. This phase of the taste was accompanied by a more perceptive appreciation of the shape and character of Chinese ornament, for the components of formalised scenes hitherto painted on surfaces acquired new character and interest in three dimensions. There was a corresponding decline of interest in English lacquer, which had grown into a flourishing industry during the last quarter of the 17th century, sufficiently important by 1700 to be protected by a 15 per cent. import duty levied on japanned and lacquered goods from the Far East. English makers, using a process that depended largely on paint and varnish, were able to provide green, yellow, vermilion, blue and cream as ground colours, and although their work lacked the brilliance and resplendent richness of the black and deep brown Oriental lacquer, and was inferior also to the products of the great French makers, such a variety of colours appealed to contemporary taste.

The Chinese taste in England and France was extended, and often confused, by the publication of plates of designs which associated oriental and rococo motifs, like the title page of Pillement's *New Book of Chinese Ornaments*, published in London in 1755 and reproduced on the opposite page. Monkeys were frequently introduced in such pseudo-Chinese compositions, and they appear in some of the plates of *A Treatise of Japanning and Varnishing*, by John Stalker and George Parker, published in 1688; the popularity of the Chinese taste may have stimulated a fashion for simian figures, carved and painted, that began in the mid-18th century and continued until the 1820s. *Reproduced by courtesy of the Victoria and Albert Museum.*

A New Book of
CHINESE ORNAMENTS
Invented & Engrav'd by P. Decker
1755.

Publish'd according to Act of Parliament 1755.

J. Pillement
sculp

See opposite page for caption.

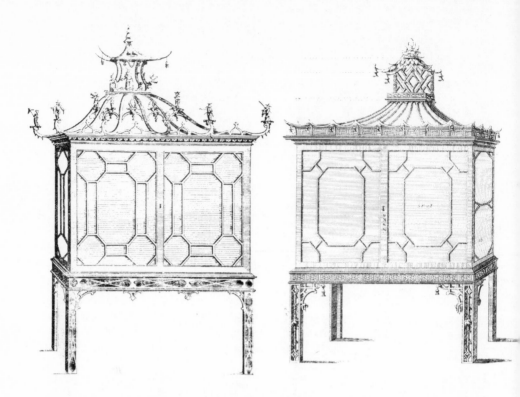

Left: China case, reproduced on a smaller scale from plate XLIX of *The Universal System of Household Furniture,* by Ince and Mayhew. *Right:* China case from plate CXXXIII of Chippendale's *Director* (first edition, 1754). Chippendale did not favour intricate elaborations of the pagoda roof motif. (See opposite page.)

From the last quarter of the 17th century to the 1730s, case furniture glowed with colour and sparkled with decoration, depicting in gold the European idea of Chinese landscapes: bird's-eye views of gardens, threaded by streams that flowed beneath steep arched bridges, diversified by temples, pavilions and pagodas, peopled by stiff little figures, and enlivened by exotic birds, blossoms and trees. This gay surface treatment appeared on cabinets, bureaux, bureau-bookcases, corner cupboards, chests with drawers and chests on stands, on mural, table, and long-case clocks, on the frames of looking-glasses and toilet glasses. Very few tables were finished in English lacquer; only a few late 17th century types with scrolled legs, and some of the later square-topped card tables with cabriole legs. After the 1740s, such formalised decoration was confined to a few surfaces, the doors and drawer fronts of

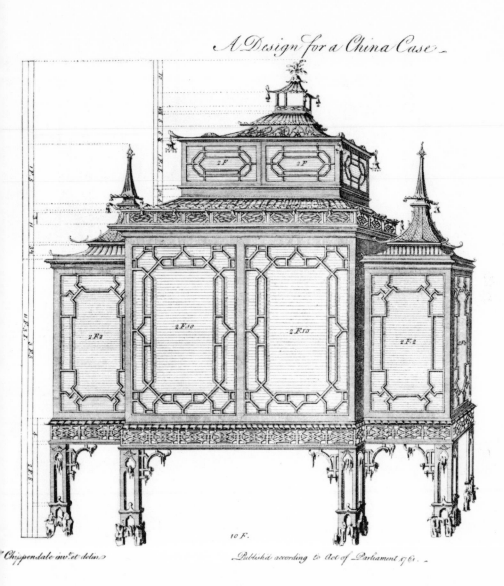

Chippendale inv.t et delin.

Publish'd according to Act of Parliament 1761.

Design for a China case, from plate CXXXVII of Chippendale's *Director* (third edition, 1762). It was described as "very proper for a Lady's Dressing-Room. It may be made of any soft Wood, and japanned any Colour." The pagoda roofs above the side cupboards are Burmese in character, though the miniature temple surmounting the central section is closer to a Chinese original.

165

Above and right: Chinese Chairs with alternative treatments for legs. From Chippendale's *Director* (first edition, 1754).

Above and left: Chinese single chairs, from Chippendale's *Director* (third edition, 1762). Compare with the designs on the opposite page and with those by Ince and Mayhew on page 169.

cabinets and commodes, and although case and seat furniture was often japanned in various hues, form now dominated colour, an ascendency illustrated by Chippendale's design for a china case, reproduced on page 165 from plate CXXXVII of the *Director*. In his note on this design, Chippendale said it "may be made of any soft Wood, and japanned any Colour". The pagoda roofs above the flanking cupboards in this example are Burmese in character, though the miniature temple surmounting the central section is closer to a Chinese original. Chippendale, and other makers, modified, exaggerated, and occasionally misrepresented oriental shapes; and the pagoda roof, as interpreted by Ince and Mayhew in their design for a china case, reproduced on page 164 from plate XLIX of *The Universal System of Household Furniture*, bears only a vestigial likeness to the Chinese pattern.

Makers of seat furniture occasionally used the pagoda motif, and showed considerable ingenuity in their use of lattice work for the backs and sides and pierced frets for the legs of chairs in the Chinese Taste. William Whitehead felt obliged to mock what he called "the present prevailing whim" when "everything is Chinese or in the Chinese taste; or as it is sometimes more modestly expressed, *partly after the Chinese manner.* Chairs, tables, chimneypieces, frames for looking-glasses, and even our most vulgar utensils, are all reduced to this new-fangled standard. . . ." His comment was published in *The World*, March 22nd, 1753, the year before Chippendale's beguiling plates of Chinese designs appeared in the first edition of the *Director*. Chippendale gave nine designs for Chinese chairs, with alternative treatments for the front legs; six are reproduced on pages 166 and 167, which closely resemble the "Gothic" chairs, on page 177. Four "Dressing Chairs" by Ince and Mayhew, opposite, are pallid renderings of Chippendale's Chinese chairs, with the exception of the oval-backed arm chair (top left), which is an uninspired example of rococo.

English furniture in the Chinese taste derived its character from an imaginative use of a few basic motifs; the style was only slightly affiliated to rococo, and the term "Chinese Chippendale", invented in the present century, is apt, for Chippendale gave substance and validity to what might otherwise have become an ephemeral fashion. No subsequent vogue for oriental design in furniture possessed the originality of the English Chinese style created by mid-Georgian carvers, cabinet-makers and upholsterers.

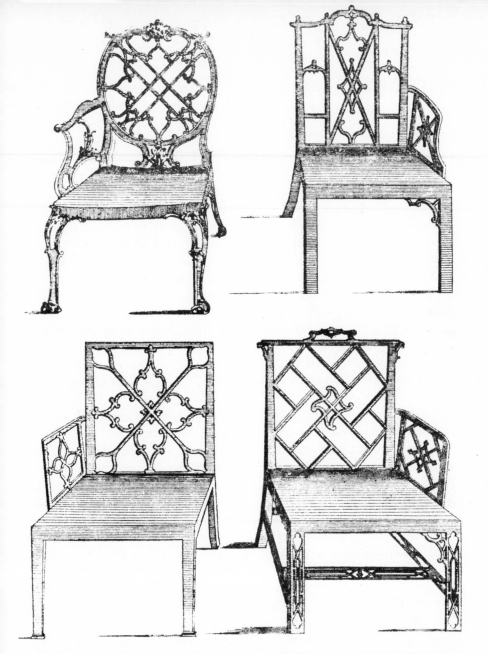

Four dressing chairs from plate XXV of *The Universal System of Household Furniture*, by Ince and Mayhew. Three of these are in the Chinese taste, but the design, top left, has rococo ornament and only a suggestion of Chinese lattice in the back. Compared with Chippendale's designs on the previous pages, these examples are uninspired.

SECTION 12. THE "GOTHICK TASTE"

Unlike the Rococo and Chinese styles, the Gothic taste that flourished in Georgian England was a native growth, though it had no continuity with the traditional Gothic, described in Section·1, which had declined in the second half of the 16th century. Georgian Gothic was a revival that reflected the antiquarian diversions of cultivated men of fashion during the mid- and late 18th century. Essentially a fashion, it lacked the vitality of a living tradition; depending on borrowed or adapted ornament and not on the spontaneous expression of a craftsman's imagination; nevertheless it was gay and amusing, not ponderously and conscientiously romantic, like the "Monastic" furniture made during the so-called "Abbotsford" period of the 1820s and '30s, or emotionally intimidating, like the work of the morally earnest Gothic revivalists in Victoria's reign. Furniture in the "Gothick" taste was as well-mannered and engagingly whimsical as the Georgian nobility and gentry and as happily innocent of high moral purpose. Sometimes that modern term, "Strawberry Hill Gothic" is used to describe such furniture when it was made in the middle years of the century, but the term is misleading for it implies that Horace Walpole was a pioneer of revived Gothic, whereas he amplified and enlivened an established fashion, generated a decade before he was born, when in 1707 the Society of Antiquaries of London was founded. That Society roused a latent interest in mediaeval art and architecture by encouraging the study of ruinous monastic buildings and churches that stood, forlorn, despoiled and neglected all over England and Wales. The viewing and recording of such remains stimulated a taste for ruins, that was soon exploited and expanded by innumerable artists and engravers. In the 1720s, Samuel and Nathaniel Buck began to publish engravings of abbeys, churches, and castles; "Bucks' Views" sold by the thousand; and their popularity led to another period of active destruction, as amateur antiquaries visited the places depicted and looted oddments of carved stone, woodwork, and fragments of shattered stained glass windows.

The incorporation of such scraps of mediaeval ornament in furniture and interior decoration was the first manifestation of the new Gothic style; and during the second quarter of the 18th century such ornamental forms became

Gothic bookcase, reproduced on a smaller scale from plate C of Chippendale's *Director* (third edition, 1762). The finials that surmount the three arched doors and continue the vertical line of the columns separating the cupboards, have affinities with rococo, which are also apparent in the slender foliations on the doors. Such exotic flourishes are in sharp contrast with the geometric sobriety of the panels in the lower part.

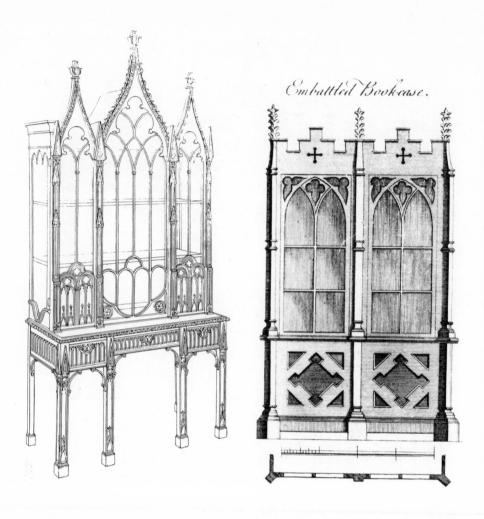

Left: Mahogany china cabinet in the Gothic taste, *circa* 1760. This is 8ft. 4 in. high, but looks higher because the elongated triangular motifs on legs and doors increase the vertical effect, and the glazing bars of the doors, branching upwards into tracery, emphasize the ascending lines of the arches' heads. *In the Victoria and Albert Museum. Right:* "Embattled Bookcase," reproduced from *Household Furniture in the Genteel Taste, for the Year 1760,* a pattern book published by "a Society of Upholsterers, Cabinet-Makers, &c.", with plates by Mathias Darly. This engraving is from plate 72 of a later edition of the book; in earlier editions it appeared on plate 69.

models for the decoration and even the shape of furniture, though that phase of the style was apparently outmoded by the 1750s, when William Whitehead, writing in *The World*, observed that "A few years ago everything was Gothic; our houses, our beds, our book-cases, and our couches, were all copied from some parts or other of our old cathedrals". (No. 12. March 22nd, 1753. Quoted from Dodsley's new edition, 1795.) All those Gothic bits and pieces had been copied and assembled with masterly tidiness by furniture-makers whose grasp of the rules and details of the classic orders of architecture ensured that no form of ornament they adapted and incorporated in their designs would erode good proportions or deny comfort.

When Whitehead dismissed Gothic as a dead or dying fashion he ignored the fresh interest kindled by the decorative experiments of Horace Walpole

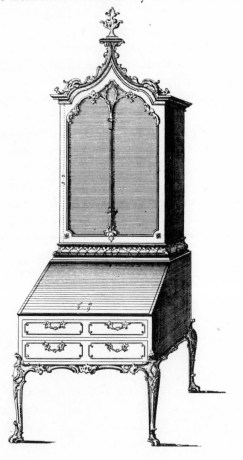

Desk and bookcase, a combination of Gothic forms and rococo ornament. Reproduced on a smaller scale from Chippendale's *Director* (third edition, 1762), plate CXI.

and his "Committee of Taste" at Strawberry Hill. "I do not mean to defend by argument a small capricious house," Walpole wrote in the preface to his *Description of Strawberry Hill*. "It was built to please my own taste and in some degree to realise my own visions." The other members of the committee were John Chute (1701–76), whom Walpole had met in Florence in 1740 and described as "an able geometrician and an exquisite architect, of the present taste, both in the Grecian and Gothick styles"; and Richard Bentley (1708–82), a gifted draughtsman and designer with a fantastic imagination. These three very different characters collaborated with amicable enthusiasm, and in the furnishing and adornment of the eastern half of Strawberry Hill, that included the dining-parlour, library, staircase, armoury and several smaller rooms, unconsciously created a new phase of the Gothic taste, which Lord Clark has aptly named Gothic Rococo. The fantastic designs of this phase represent the so-called "Strawberry Hill Gothic", but were wholly different in character from the furniture illustrated in contemporary copy books. Chippendale associated rococo and Chinese ornament with Gothic; the three chairs reproduced on page 177 from plate XXV of the *Director* (third edition, 1762) show an odd amalgamation of motifs; the hall chair, from plate XVII, on page 176, with interlaced pointed arches in the back, is a more emphatic expression of the Gothic taste, and the country-made mahogany elbow chair beside it with the three conjoined lancet arches in the back is a simpler interpretation of the fashion.

Chippendale's designs for a desk and bookcase on a frame, from plate CXI, on page 173, represent another uneasy association of Gothic and rococo; but the bookcase, from plate C reproduced on page 171, is a more harmonious example of Gothic rococo. Makers and patrons alike were attracted by the pointed arch, and like the pagoda roof motif in the Chinese style, variations of this feature often determined the shape of case furniture and chair backs. The Gothic bookcase on page 171 shows the dominating influence of the pointed arch, though not to the same extent as the mahogany china cabinet on page 172, where the arch appears as a recurrent motif on legs, drawer fronts, glazing bars, and the door heads which form a trio of elegant arches, laced with delicate carving, each crowned by a bold finial. This design owes nothing to the copy books of makers like Chippendale or Ince and Mayhew, nor to those issued by Batty Langley and others who attempted to regularise Gothic. Langley's five Gothic "Orders" were condemned by Horace Walpole who said: "All that his books achieved, has been to teach carpenters to massacre that venerable species. . . ." (*Anecdotes*

Library table in mahogany with green leather top. This probably stood in the library of the Gothic house, designed by Sanderson Miller for the Countess of Pomfret in 1760. *Reproduced by courtesy of Leeds City Art Gallery and Temple Newsam House.*

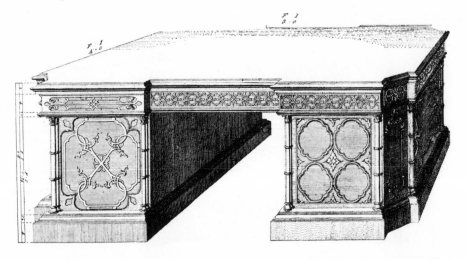

Library table, reproduced from plate LXXXV of Chippendale's *Director* (third edition, 1762). Described as "A Gothic Library-Table. The corners are canted with proper Breaks, and three-quarter Pillars fixed to the edges of the Doors, and they open with them". Alternative designs are given for the ornament on the pedestals and the frieze.

of Painting in England. Quoted from the third edition, printed for J. Dodsley, 1786. Vol. IV, page 226.)

Many pieces of mid-18th century furniture in the Gothic taste were components of some interior, furnished and decorated in the style, like the mahogany table on page 175 which probably stood in the library of "Pomfret Castle", the Gothic house in Arlington Street designed in 1760 by Sanderson Miller for the Countess of Pomfret. It is now in the collection at Temple Newsam House, Leeds. Miller may well have designed the table, which, in general form resembles one in Chippendale's *Director*, reproduced on the same page. Chippendale's alternative treatments for pedestal panels and frieze have a staid regularity, very different from the lively, sparkling ornament of the Temple Newsam table. In that example attached columns rise from floor level to desk top, relieving the massive character of the design, whereas

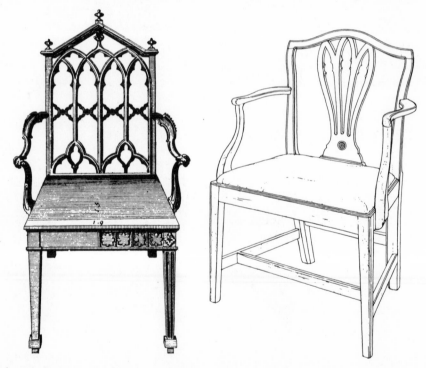

Left: A hall chair, with Gothic tracery in the back and the top rail surmounted by three finials. From plate XXV of Chippendale's *Director* (third edition, 1762). *Right:* Elbow chair in mahogany with slip seat, *circa* 1765–1770. The triple-lancet splat is a country maker's acknowledgement of the Gothic taste. *In the author's possession.*

Three Gothic chairs from plate XXV of Chippendale's *Director* (third edition, 1762). The "Gothic" features are difficult to detect: the designs have the same decorative characteristics as the Chinese chairs on pages 166 and 167.

177

Chippendale accentuates that character by the solidity of plinth and frieze. In both tables the form and moulded detail are regulated by regard for the proportions of classic architecture, though the architectural relationship is more marked in Chippendale's design where columns, ascending from the plinth, support an entablature deep enough to accommodate spacious drawers.

Ince and Mayhew gave only three plates to Gothic subjects in *The Universal System of Household Furniture*, that was issued serially between 1759 and 1762, when the third edition of Chippendale's *Director* was also appearing in separate parts before publication in book form. One of their plates, LXXXVI,

Alternative treatments for a Gothic chimneypiece, reproduced on a smaller scale from plate LXXXVI of *The Universal System of Household Furniture*, by Ince and Mayhew (1759–62). The designers have produced an amalgam of Gothic and rococo motifs: exuberant, extravagant, but not ill-proportioned. Compare this design with the sober interpretation of the Gothic taste on the opposite page.

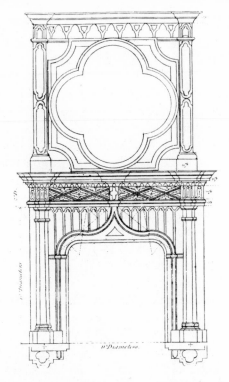

Gothic chimneypiece, from plate 85 of *The Builder's Companion*, by William Pain (London: 1769). Pain described himself as an architect and joiner, or architect and carpenter. This design has a classical orderliness, and none of the fancifulness of ornamentalists like Ince and Mayhew. (See opposite page.)

reproduced opposite, shows alternative decoration for a chimneypiece, with rococo and Gothic ornament intermingled. A far more restrained design for a Gothic chimneypiece was given by William Pain in *The Builder's Companion* (1769), and this example, which owed something to Batty Langley's copy books, is shown above. The Gothic taste persisted throughout the second half of the 18th century, and far into the 19th; but by then it had passed into a romantic and picturesque phase; the gaiety and good manners of Gothic rococo were lost; and when the rules and proportions of classic architecture were disowned alike by patrons and makers, old graces were replaced by the chaos of the "Abbotsford" period.

SECTION 13. THE LOUIS XVI AND DIRECTOIRE STYLES

A two-way traffic in ideas about furniture design had long existed between France and England; openly acknowledged by English makers who were quite frank about their borrowings, and never hesitated to say that this or that article was "in the French taste". No comparable acknowledgment was made in France to English sources of inspiration; not because of a narrow artistic isolationism, but because designers and patrons in both countries were aware that France originated ideas and England adapted them, and only rarely was this practice reversed, as for example in the Neo-Classic style, La Pompadour's legacy to national taste, which owed more to the work of Robert Adam than was ever admitted or even suspected by French society. The taste of her successor, Jeanne, Comtesse du Barry was very different; the restraint and orderliness of Neo-Classic which replaced the creative audacity of rococo was followed by a style that was still orderly, for classic architecture remained in control of proportions, but delicate formality gave way to an excessive, almost intimidating use of rich materials. Nothing in England was comparable with the furnishing and interior treatment of Madame du Barry's Château de Louveciennes or the pavilion designed by Ledoux near the main building; this was an example of the Neo-Classic style in a new, affluent phase. A chimneypiece of carved lapis lazuli in one of the small salons was reflected by walls sheathed by mirrors; the ceiling was adorned by a painting called "Country Amusements", an allegory of love; bronze and gold ornament shone everywhere, and the curves and convolutions of the furniture, less fragile than rococo, delighted the cultivated, charming and useless society that approved and imitated the taste of the last of "the left-hand Queens of France", whose reign ended when Louis XVI's began.

Compared with that extravagant prelude, the Louis XVI style had an opulent placidity: although luxury was organised as it had never been organised before, although the number of convenient articles was multiplied, and rare materials and precious metals were used with triumphant skill, the curvilinear conception of design was abandoned; cabinet-makers reverted to the use of rectilinear shapes; refined simplicity of form gave a static, imper-

Louis XVI secretaire, veneered with satinwood, purple-wood and sycamore on oak. On the drop-front two rectangular placques of blue *oeil-de-perdrix* Sèvres porcelain are mounted, each painted with a bouquet of flowers. The plaques are framed with enriched gilt bronze mouldings. The fluted angle columns flanking the drop-front are set in coved recesses, with capitals and bases of gilt bronze. The mouldings are flatter and plainer than in the Louis XV style, faithfully following classical sections without any fanciful variations and additions; the discipline of architectural proportions, never quite lost, have now been fully restored to furniture design. *In the Wallace Collection.*

Salon in the Louis XVI style. The creative audacity of rococo has been superseded by a placid opulence, with gold gleaming on mouldings and ornamental details. Luxury has been organised as luxury had never been organised before; the proportions of the background are determined by architectural rules; the furniture shows a resumption of rectilinear design, though curves are not discarded. From Maison de Campagne de Mme H. Blanquefort. (Gironde.)

sonal air to furniture, a geometric rigidity that enhanced the decorative quality of materials and the intricacy of inlaid ornament. Mouldings were used sparingly; flatter in section, but still based on classical prototypes, they suggested uniformity; the suppression of gay and fanciful effects enhanced the exquisite proportions of furniture, and sobriety of line and the faultless unity of vertical and horizontal elements created an impression of calm grace that gave no hint of the social turbulence which influenced the choice of ornament towards the end of the reign: in maturity, the style reflected the sublime complacency of the Court and of French society.

The art of cabinet-making had reached its highest level in mid-18th century France; little remained to be discovered in the handling of traditional materials, but innovations in the association of wood and metal and porcelain,

Bedroom in the Louis XVI style. Mouldings are flatter in section, though, like those in the salon on the opposite page, are based on classical prototypes; but this interior exhibits a sobriety of line, a restraint in the use of ornament, and gives an impression of calm grace; gaiety is muted, and everything suggests order and stability, a complete visual denial of the social turbulence that seethed outside the royal palaces and great houses of the nobility, in cities and countryside. From Hôtel Baour â Bordeaux.

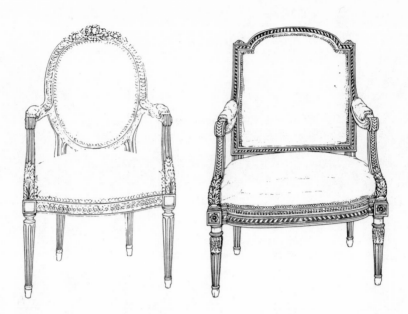

Left: One of a pair of arm-chairs, with beech frames, lightly carved and gilt, and oval backs. Compare with the chair of Adam design on page 194. *Right:* Arm-chair with square back and beech frame, gilt, with carved cable moulding round the back and seats. One of a set, upholstered in Beauvais tapestry. *In the Wallace Collection.*

already practised in the previous reign, were now enlivened by an adventurous and experimental spirit. Native and foreign woods were used, particularly mahogany, for which there was a vogue in the early phases of the style; the parquetry in Marie Antoinette's boudoir at Fontainebleau was in mahogany, and finely figured veneers of that wood were used on an oak ground for large surfaces on chests and cabinets. Bands and small plaques of brass and gilded bronze were inlaid in wood, and in addition to panels and plaques of Sèvres china let into the panels of case furniture, bas-reliefs of Wedgwood on a blue ground came into fashion. The secretaire on page 181 illustrates the variety of materials used for the decoration of a relatively simple design. Experiments with materials were not confined to decorative work: cast-iron was occasionally used to replace wood, and a pair of tables in that material, toned to a dark green, are in the Wallace Collection.

Ornamentalists still relied largely on antique ornament, editing and employing classic prototypes from Greek and Roman art and architecture

Sofa with lightly carved gilt frame, the back surmounted by cresting in the form of a wreath, ribbons, and leaves. Like the chairs opposite, the seat and back are upholstered in Beauvais tapestry. (The pattern is not shown in the drawing.) All three examples show the sobriety of line and stability characteristic of Louis XVI seat furniture. *In the Wallace Collection.*

with consummate skill, but presently these were supplemented from sources far older, and the sphinxes and hawk-headed or jackal-headed gods of Ancient Egypt began to appear in French decorative art, anticipating a fashion that was later inspired by Napoleon's unfortunate Egyptian campaign. The French Empire style was generated in the reign of Louis XVI, and during the last troubled years of that reign the influence of political demagogues invaded the realm of taste. Revolutionary symbols masqueraded as ornament: workmen's tools, and such articles as the spirit-level, representing *equality*; clasped hands, *fraternity*; the Phrygian cap, *Liberty recovered*; and pikes, *the freedom of man*: such allegories were a modish acknowledgement of change that had not yet erupted into violence, solemn expressions of political faith, short-lived for they were hopelessly incompatible with French love of gaiety. The Louis XVI style was the last magnificent declaration of aristocratic taste; thereafter patronage was usurped by a new rich class; though cabinet-makers, trained under the monarchy, managed to preserve continuity in classic design, when the luxury trades came to life again after the Terror.

Table with rectangular top of red Egyptian porphyry, with four tapered and fluted legs, surmounted by Ionic capitals of bronze, chased and gilt. Writing slides, fitted below the top, may be pulled out at each end. *In the Wallace Collection.*

The Directoire style, named after the Directorate that governed France before Napoleon controlled the country, was a simplified version of Louis XVI design, economically executed, for the prodigal spending that came so naturally and gracefully to aristocrats, frightened the upstarts who had made their money during and after the Revolution and to whom wealth was a new and slightly alarming experience. Furniture was still well-designed, for artist-craftsmen, like architects, retained their loyalty to the classic orders and to classic ornament; it was well-made, but cheaper materials were used, brass instead of bronze; the subtle refinements of cabinet-making were missing; the angularity of case furniture was unmodified by judicious curves while mean-ness in execution and a slavish and rather nervous imitation of the antique suggested the social and cultural instability of a class anxious to avoid vul-garity but also anxious to exhibit the evidence of their unaccustomed

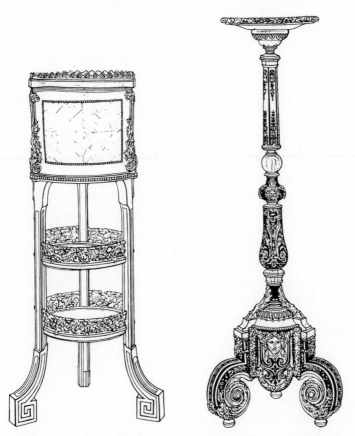

Two late 18th century guéridons, which illustrate the considerable variation in the form. The example on the right preserves some of the original character of the guéridon, which was primarily a lamp support; but was transformed into the guéridon table. (See page 126.) *Both examples are in the Wallace Collection.*

prosperity. The only conspicuous innovation was the introduction of so-called Etruscan decorative features and ornamental details. Chairs with swept, concave legs and scrolled backs, comparable with but clumsier than the chairs of the English Greek Revival; seats with X-shaped underframing; day-beds with scrolled ends; and case furniture veneered in mahogany, for a reddish-brown variety of that wood was used not only for furniture, but for pilasters on walls and for doors, and door and window architraves. This style flourished in the last days of the Republic and formed a comparatively modest introduction to the far more grandiose Empire style of the early 19th century.

SECTION 14. THE ADAM, NEO-CLASSICAL STYLE

The last three decades of the 18th century in England were distinguished by a style that became identified with national taste; that style was created by Robert Adam (1728–92), and inspired by his sensitive and refined rendering of classic architecture and ornament. Adam's reinterpretation of the classic idiom followed his diligent study of antique remains in Italy, where he lived from 1754 to 1757, spending some part of his time in Dalmatia where he made a detailed record of the well-preserved ruins of Diocletian's Palace at Spalato. Like Kent before him, Adam accepted an over-all responsibility for the design of buildings, interior decoration and all the components of furnishing, not only chairs, tables, sideboards, beds, cabinets, presses, chimney glasses, girandoles, chandeliers and lanterns, but curtains, carpets, fireplaces, grates, fire-irons, fenders, door knockers and key-plates, upon which he impressed the delicate characteristics of the Neo-Classic taste. He began his career as a furniture designer about 1762, when the Seven Years' War was ending. The preliminaries of the Peace of Paris were signed in the November of that year, and in 1763 relations between France and England were resumed, so the English nobility and gentry could again travel to the French capital, where they were delighted by the new and relatively orderly Neo-Classical style that was far more congenial to their taste than rococo. They were also attracted by the vogue for articles *à la grecque*, which was then exciting the interest of French society. This French fashion may have been one of the contributory influences that originated the Grecian and neo-Greek revivals in the early 1760s, though those revivals were animated chiefly by the publication in 1762 of the first volume of *The Antiquities of Athens,* by James ("Athenian") Stuart and Nicholas Revett. The subsequent development of the neo-Greek style owed little to French influence, though the French and English neo-classical styles at first developed on similar lines.

Robert Adam had visited France in 1754, and although he never went there again he could not have been unaware of a French furniture style that corresponded so closely to his own. Early examples of English Neo-Classical furniture were visibly indebted to contemporary French taste, especially when Adam transformed the character of gilded furniture, an achievement

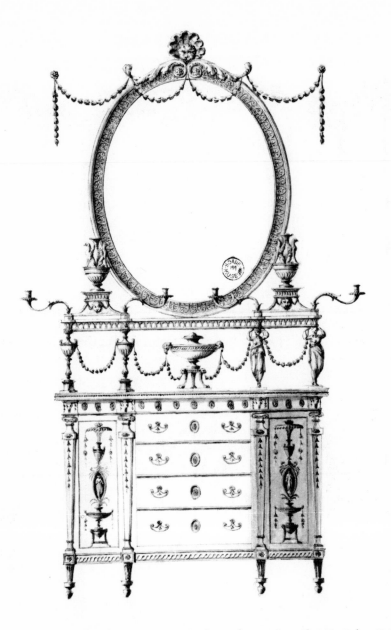

Design for a glass frame and commode, by Robert Adam for Sir John Griffin.
Reproduced from the original drawing, dated November 1778. *By courtesy of the
Trustees of Sir John Soane's Museum.*

189

Sideboard table reproduced on a smaller scale from *The Cabinet-Maker and Uphol-sterers' Guide*, a book of some 300 designs "from drawings by A. Hepplewhite and Co., Cabinet-Makers", published in 1788, two years after George Hepplewhite's death. The ornamental details show the influence of Robert Adam.

Serpentine-fronted sideboard with deep cupboards on either side and three drawers. The fan device, often used by Adam, is inlaid in the spandrels that flank the central opening; the Marlboro' legs are fluted. Reproduced from Hepplewhite's *Guide*.

One of a pair of marble-topped side tables designed by Robert Adam, 1756. Formerly in the Long Gallery at Croome Court, Worcestershire, and now in the Philadelphia Museum of Art.

that prompted Horace Walpole to observe that "Adam, our most admired, is all gingerbread, filigraine, and fan-painting". (Letter to Sir Horace Mann, April 22nd, 1775). Gingerbread meant gilding, for the gingerbread cakes sold at fairs were always brightened with imitation gold leaf. Apart from changing the character of gilded furniture and increasing the demand for it, Adam's discreet use of lightly carved and painted ornament gave greater elegance to furniture, his introduction of shield-shaped, oval and lyre backs brought new graces to chairs; and in the mature phase of his style, from the end of the 1760s to the beginning of the 1780s, his taste began to influence many contemporary makers. The extent of his influence was later recorded in such copy books as *The Cabinet-Maker and Upholsterers' Guide,* published in 1788 by George Hepplewhite's widow, two years after her husband's death, and was visible, too, though to a lesser extent, in the designs of Thomas Shearer in *The Cabinet-Makers' London Book of Prices,* also issued in 1788; and clearly marked by many examples in *The Cabinet-Maker and Upholsterers' Drawing Book,* that Thomas Sheraton issued in four parts between 1791 and 1794 before finally publishing it in book form.

The Adam style replaced the robust, assertive and essentially masculine air of the mid-Georgian interior and its furnishing; for his style had a feminine quality, not frivolously feminine like the last phase of rococo, but well-bred, ladylike and restrained. The form of furniture became slender but not too slender, and never flimsy; mouldings were lighter in section, even the glazing bars of sash windows were reduced to an almost knife-edge slimness; caned seats were reintroduced on chairs; buttoned upholstery appeared; mahogany was still the chief material, though satinwood and exotic timbers were occasionally used, and japanned and painted furniture was associated with chairs and pier tables and looking-glass frames that gleamed with gilding. By the last decade of the century there were, it has been estimated, over a hundred and fifty carvers and gilders in business in London alone, as well as specialists in water gilding. *Continued on page 198*

Left: Mahogany chest of drawers, carved and gilt, with rams' heads at the upper corners and hoof feet below. The front has a shallow serpentine curve, and the sides are curved. Gadrooning is carved on the edge of the top. The delicate ornament, derived from antique sources and skilfully disposed, is typical of the neo-classic style that Robert Adam perfected. *Right:* Carved, painted and gilt pedestal, with the ornament on the tapering panels carved in low relief.

Above, left: Carved and painted three branch wall light. Like the other examples of the Adam neo-classical style on this page and opposite, the design illustrates a fresh and inventive approach to the use and placing of antique ornament. *Above, right:* Posted bed in kingwood with spiral turning on the posts. The frieze of the tester has a Greek key pattern with a central tablet, painted with classical figures. *Circa* 1760. *Formerly in the possession of the late Robert Atkinson, F.R.I.B.A.*

Above, left: Armchair designed by Robert Adam. *Circa* 1777. The frame is lightly carved and gilded, and the oval back is supported by the upraised wings of recumbent sphinxes. Compare this with the French oval-backed chair on page 184. *Right:* Lyre-backed single chair, one of a set. Both examples are from Osterley Park, Middlesex. *Reproduced by courtesy of the Victoria and Albert Museum.*

Right: Single chair with painted frame and caned oval back and dipped seat. *Formerly in the possession of Miss Muriel Barron.*

Bar back settee reproduced on a smaller scale from Hepplewhite's *Guide* (1788). The conjoined shield-backs form a serpentine top rail.

Above, left: Shield back single chair reproduced on a smaller scale from Hepplewhite's *Guide. Right:* Low-back Windsor chair in mahogany, *circa* 1760–70. Fashionable makers produced these elegant variations of the Windsor type. This is drawn from one of a set of six at Ham House, Petersham, Surrey. *Reproduced by courtesy of the Victoria and Albert Museum.*

Right: Easy chair, described by Hepplewhite as a "Saddle Cheek", and reproduced on a slightly smaller scale from the *Guide* (1788). The name is derived from the shape of the wings, which suggest the outline of a saddle. This is a rather clumsy variation on the form of the winged easy chair established in the late 17th century. Compare with those illustrated on pages 111 and 142.

A duchesse, reproduced from Hepplewhite's *Guide*. This consists of two tub-backed easy chairs, with padded arms, and a stool between them, the whole forming a double-ended day-bed. Such composite chairs and stools were used in France and England during and after the middle years of the 18th century with little difference in their basic design. Compare with the French example on page 125.

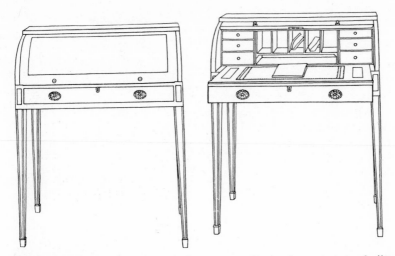

The Marlboro' leg, so inelegantly depicted in Hepplewhite's engraving of a "Saddle Cheek" opposite, was a slender, tapering leg of square-section, like those on the writing desks on this page. *Above:* A desk in mahogany inlaid with lines of satin-wood, which has a cylinder fall. *Circa* 1790–1800.

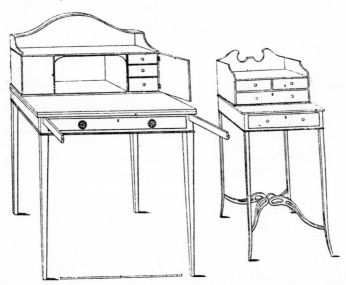

Left: A lady's writing cabinet, for which the contemporary term sheveret was used. (This name appears in the Gillow records for desks of this type.) *Right:* A miniature sheveret or lady's work table. Both designs reproduced on a smaller scale from plate 7 of *The Prices of Cabinet Work* (1797 edition).

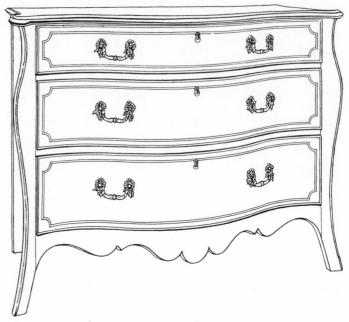

Chest of drawers in mahogany with serpentine front and French feet. The top drawer is fitted with a sliding looking-glass, and fittings for toilet articles. *Circa* 1770–80. *In the Victoria and Albert Museum.*

At some time during the 1770s, the cellaret sideboard with drawers and cupboards was invented, and this invention is often attributed to Thomas Shearer; two variations of the design appeared, signed by him on plate 5 of *The Cabinet-Makers' London Book of Prices*, one of them bow-fronted, the other serpentine-fronted, both with the square-sectioned tapering legs, known in the trade as Marlboro', and used on various types of tables and chairs. But Shearer may have recorded a type already well-established among makers. The serpentine-fronted sideboard reproduced from Hepplewhite's *Guide* on page 190 has fluted Marlboro' legs, with thermed or spade feet, and the influence of Adam's classical taste is apparent in the slender scrolls on the central drawer-front, the inlaid fan ornament of the spandrels below that drawer, and the husks that decorate the vertical divisions. The sideboard table, on the same page, is described in the *Guide* as a sideboard, for by the 1780s the terms were apparently interchangeable: that example might well be one of Adam's own designs, and owes far more to the educated taste of an architect than to the skill and ingenuity of a cabinet-maker. Sideboard tables of comparable design were often flanked by pedestals, supporting urn-shaped knife cases; and a little later the pedestal sideboard was introduced, with the pedestals attached to each end of the sideboard.

Although makers were required to interpret the designs of architects and other men of taste, the demands made on their skill were never overtly extravagant; on paper the fragility of some of Adam's designs might seem exaggerated, and many of his original drawings in the collection at Sir John Soane's Museum represent stimulating challenges to the carver and gilder, such as the design for an oval glass frame and commode for Sir John Griffin (1778), shown on page 189. Like all Adam's work these examples reveal the light touch of an inexhaustible fancy; engaging, fantastic though never too intricate, always reanimating antique ornament without loss of respect for the Roman prototypes. Such fabulous creatures as the chimera, griffin and sphinx, long favoured by ornamentalists and carvers, were tamed and trimmed and endowed with a formal and slightly frigid dignity; especially the sphinx, which in the 1770s was used both in France and England, though French designers favoured the ancient Egyptian form, and Adam and his contemporaries the Grecian. The oval back of the armchair from Osterley Park, Middlesex, shown on page 194, is supported by recumbent sphinxes. (Com-

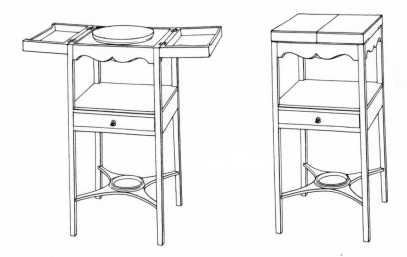

Basin stand in mahogany, with drawer below central shelf and a lower shelf for a ewer. The scale of ablutions in the late 18th century may be judged from the diminutive basin, but the compact elegance of the design is undeniable. *Circa* 1780–90.

Nest of tables in mahogany, *circa* 1790. The slender turned legs were known as "spider-legs", but that is probably not a contemporary term.

pare the design of that armchair with the oval-backed Louis XVI on page 184; French and English fashions were *en rapport*, though national sovereignty in taste was never surrendered.)

The side table, pedestal, chest and wall light on pages 191, 192 and 193, exemplify the ornamental felicity of the Adam style; an architectural orderliness controls the proportions and embellishment of each design; carving, gilding and painted decoration unite gaiety with formality, as they are united in a ballet. Robert Adam employed such artists as Pergolesi, Cipriani, Zucchi and his wife, Angelica Kaufmann, to adorn with their delicate paintings the furniture and the interiors of the houses he designed and furnished. In the hands of designers less skilled than Robert Adam furniture occasionally became attenuated; some of the reassuring stability that characterised the early and mid-Georgian period was diminished, but such flirtations with flimsiness were indulged in largely by Victorian imitators of the Adam style, which they seldom understood as their approach was that of the copyist. By the close of the 18th century furniture had a rigidity of line, relieved only in case furniture by bow or serpentine fronts; the Marlboro' leg, sturdy or slender, lacked the grace of the cabriole type; and designers seemed to be committed to angulated shapes; curves were so slight as to be barely perceptible, until in the last decade a new curvilinear revolution prepared the way for the final graces of the Georgian age.

SECTION 15. THE FRENCH EMPIRE STYLE AND ITS SUCCESSORS

The French Empire style has been described as heroic, possibly because it was uncompromisingly masculine, frigidly majestic, devoid of gaiety and austerely detached from the intimacies of life. Even concessions to comfort were rejected if they happened to conflict with the rather bleak conception of abstract beauty favoured by designers, though the increasing influence of upholsterers counteracted this tendency in seat furniture. Certainly it was the last distinctive French style, and although it bequeathed some of its severely classical character to the styles of the Restoration and Louis-Philippe, those styles never conveyed a comparable air of dignity and orderliness. Empire furniture had a tenuous continuity with that of the monarchy, for the cult of antiquity, so closely associated with the Louis XVI style, was approved by the revolutionary generation, and fortunately the ornamental symbols of political change did not survive the savage realities of the Terror. Nobody desired to perpetuate the taste of the Directorate plutocrats. That was swept away by Napoleon's rise to power, and new standards of taste were imposed, controlled as always in France by an infallible sense of style and by consistent loyalty to the classic idiom. A fresh, virile spirit informed the work of artist-craftsmen, which owed something to the erudition of archaeologists, but far more to the art of Charles Percier and Pierre Fontaine, two gifted architects and designers who, in partnership, perfected the Empire style.

Napoleon's expedition to Egypt had included a team of archaeologists, and the full and scholarly record of antiquities made by those savants revived a latent interest in Egyptian art and architecture. Men like Vivant Denon, an architect and archaeologist, who had accompanied the expedition, helped to create a style that was different in quality and character from the transitory fashion for Egyptian ornament in Louis XVI's reign, for it was derived from knowledge of the originals, though the employment of royal and sacred symbols for mere decoration would have outraged the pharaohs and priests of ancient Egypt. The sphinx reappeared; the uraeus, that serpent emblem of gods and kings, became a favourite motif; while the figures of Isis and those grotesque divinities with the heads of birds or animals on human bodies

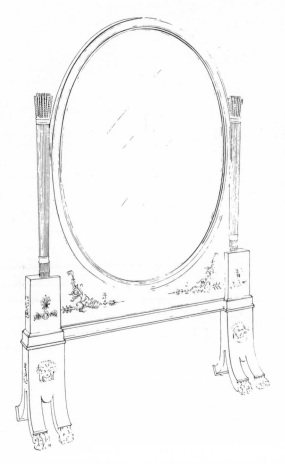

Cheval glass, mahogany with ormolu mounts, gilt. A similar example is at Malmaison. This is typical of the more restrained manifestations of the French Empire Style.

adorned the surfaces of beds and case furniture, also table legs and the arms and legs of chairs. The Greek caryatid frequently supported the tops of console and occasional tables, but the original form, a woman acting as a pillar, was often changed into a semi-human shape, with a female head and bust emerging from the upper part of a quadrangular shaft which rested on human feet; a mixture saved from absurdity by good proportions. Other ornamental eccentricities included the monopodium, formed from the head, chest and leg of a lion, or some fanciful hybrid such as an eagle-headed chimera or a winged sphinx.

Two examples of the use of the caryatid motif. *Above:* Console table in mahogany with bronze mounts, gilt. The feet that emerge from the bottom of the tapering quadrangular shafts imply a grotesque elongation and compression of the figures which join them to the heads. Variations of this device were used in England during the Regency period. (See page 214.) *Below:* Chest of drawers in mahogany, with bronze mounts. Both designs are about 1800.

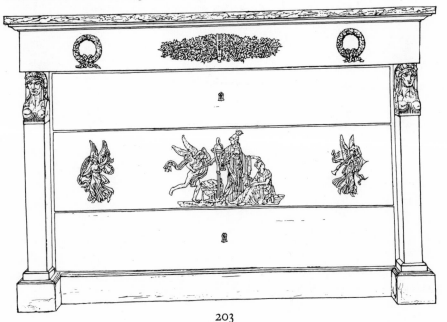

Ruddy brown or very dark mahogany was used, occasionally rosewood, with the surfaces highly polished. The tables, cabinets, writing desks, graceful scroll-ended beds, and the frames of large cheval glasses, were ornamented chiefly by applied metalwork, flat gilt ormolu mounts that reproduced Greek, Roman or Egyptian motifs, discreetly placed and used with moderation. Mouldings were used sparingly, carved decoration hardly ever, though the vertical members of cheval glass frames were sometimes fluted. Symbols of war and victory asserted the martial spirit of the times and satisfied the personal taste and the political policy of the Emperor, for Napoleon, though usually indifferent to his surroundings, liked them to convey an atmosphere of triumphant power and luxury. So beds were designed to look like tents, with hangings held up by bronze pikes; cylindrical stools of yellow hide were corded like drums; and trophies of arms were assembled with Greek and Roman helmets, shields, spears, swords and flags arranged in highly decorative but slightly intimidating compositions. French designers knew how to civilise camp manners; even in the light-headed days of Louis XV they had never allowed furniture to become ridiculous, and such military manifestations of the Empire style never became outrageously incongruous.

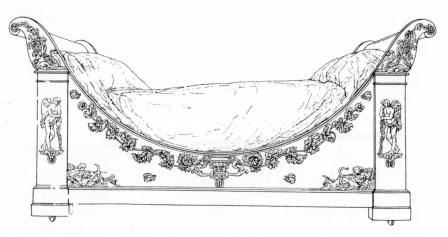

Bed in mahogany with rising scrolled ends. The bronze mounts are gilt. *Circa* 1800. Like the cheval glass on page 202 and the chest of drawers on page 203, the use of ornament is restrained, and confined to naturalistic and classical subjects: at that date the decoration of furniture had not yet become a vehicle for military glory.

Fall-front writing desk in mahogany, with bronze mounts, gilt; supported in front on bold and rather heavy paw feet. The entasis on the flanking columns is exaggerated, and the columns taper towards the base. *In the possession of Maureen Stafford.*

Empire seat furniture lacked the elegance of 18th century design: it was massive, richly upholstered and often very comfortable. Armchairs borrowed ornamental features from ancient Greek ceremonial seats; winged chimeras, sphinxes or swans supported the padded arms, and the swan motif persisted, bereft of wings, the beak pointing downwards and the long neck looped and merging into a scroll just above the seat rail, like the example on page 208. The other chairs on that page and the day-beds on page 209, show how the characteristic shapes and ornament of the Empire style preserved their intrinsic vitality in the succeeding periods, for the style, like the memory of French military supremacy, survived until the middle of the century. The reactionary Bourbons, who seemed to think that their return to the French throne implied the return of the 18th century, were unable to exert more than a superficial influence on taste. This was manifested by a lifeless revival of the monarchial styles, when furniture of the Louis XIV, XV, and XVI periods was copied, for the most part rather badly; even earlier periods were raided for ideas, and imitations of Gothic and Renaissance furniture became intermittently fashionable, though the former had none of the whimsicality of

English Georgian Gothic or the fervour of the Gothic revival. French Gothic furniture of the 1830s and '40s was not the culmination of a long-cultivated form of antiquarian taste that had grown up in a civilised manner within a classical framework; no equivalent of Horace Walpole or Sanderson Miller had supervised its development. The taste for Gothic during the fourth and fifth decades of the 19th century was fostered partly by literary influence, and owed something to the popularity of Victor Hugo's *Notre Dame de Paris*, that was published in 1831. The so-called "Cathedral" and "Troubador" styles reflected an expanding interest in the Middle Ages, as in Britain the influence of Sir Walter Scott's mediaeval romances was reflected by the pseudo-Gothic furniture that was later described as "Abbotsford", and by the "Monastic" style that flourished at the same time as French Gothic. Furniture designers made no attempt to revive and continue the authentic Gothic tradition of the late 15th and early 16th centuries, and contented themselves with such simplified forms as the arches and apertures that appear in the back of the chair on page 208, or with fragments of tracery, and architectural features like finials and crockets. Only furniture made in the countryside gave evidence of a robust continuity with the past, for country makers, while occasionally acknowledging the existence of contemporary fashions, preserved their own methods of construction, used familiar materials, and still carved ornament on mouldings and surfaces in the manner of their 16th and 17th century predecessors.

In the 1830s and '40s, furniture was again decorated with carved ornament; scrolls and foliations like those on the cupboard opposite were, by comparison with earlier examples, blunted and coarsely executed. Geometric frets, and turned work reappeared, while the clarity of classic ornamental motifs diminished. Designers seemed to be losing the infallible sense of proportion that had for two centuries controlled the character of French furniture. The partial loss of that sense may have been due to the increasing influence of upholsterers, who now determined the shape of nearly all types of seat furniture, with the result that the frame sometimes completely disappeared, as on the chair on page 210, or was subordinated to buttoned upholstery, as exemplified by the settee on the same page.

The creative impulse that had sustained French leadership in furniture design since the mid-17th century, had been lost by the mid-19th; and over three hundred years of original achievement in a not inconsiderable art was temporarily submerged by the wave of bad taste that washed over European civilisation.

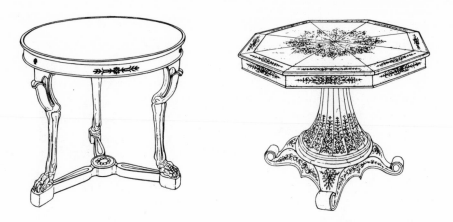

Left: Circular table, supported on three lions' legs, with inlaid marquetry ornament in the frieze. An example of the survival of the Empire style in the second quarter of the century. *Right:* Table with octagonal top supported on a facetted pillar that broadens out towards the base with scrolled feet below. The surfaces are inlaid with marquetry.

Left: Sideboard table with two tiers and turned front supports. 1830–40. *Right:* Glass-fronted cupboard, with carved superstructure. The carved ornament is bluntly executed and lacks the delicate precision of earlier periods. 1840–50.

Left: Elbow chair with scrolled arms, deeply cushioned seat, and upholstered panel in the back. The influence of the upholsterer on the design is slight. 1815–25. *Centre:* Armchair with padded arms and buttoned upholstery. The swan-neck motif has survived from the Empire period. 1830–40. *Right:* Arc-back round-seated chair, with turned and fluted front legs on castors and marquetry ornament inlaid on the seat rail. 1840–50.

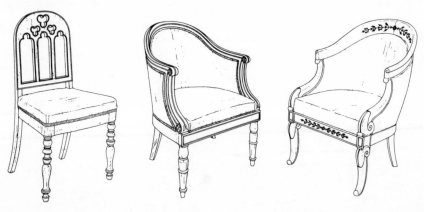

Left: Single chair with turned front legs and a pierced back in the Gothic taste. 1830–40. *Centre:* Tub chair with turned front legs. 1830–40. The lines of the back retain the graces of the Empire style. *Right:* Tub chair that projects the characteristics of the Empire style into the second quarter of the century. Seat rail and top rail of back are inlaid with marquetry.

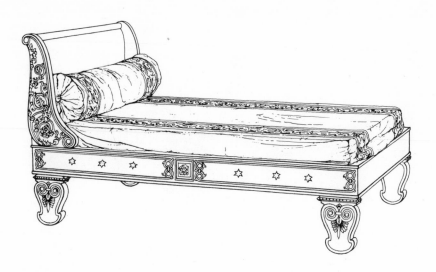

Day-bed, Restoration period, but with the characteristic classic ornamental details of the Empire style, and outward-curving scrolled head.

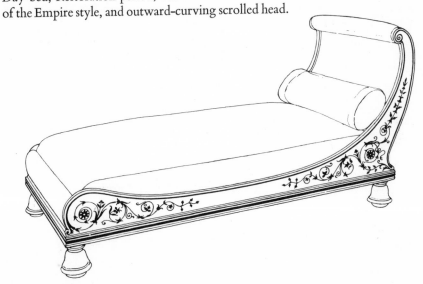

Day-bed, with the elongated curves delicately emphasised by marquetry ornament, supported on bell feet. The influence of the Empire style survived into the 1830s, and is apparent in this design, though the shape is lighter and more refined than the day-bed at the top of the page.

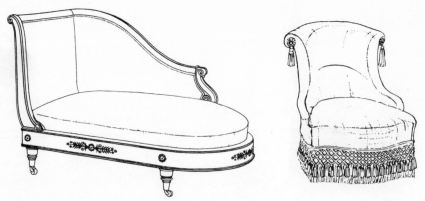

Left: Semi-settee with rounded end and turned legs mounted on castors. The broad seat frame is inlaid with marquetry. Such light, modestly ornamented designs appeared in the 1820s. The frame-maker had not yet abdicated in favour of the upholsterer. *Right:* This easy chair shows how at the end of the Louis-Philippe period the upholsterer had gained control of the design of seat furniture. No sign of a frame appears; fringes and tassels below the seat conceal the legs, and the arms have become vestigial.

The upholsterer has determined the character of this Louis-Philippe settee. The fluting on the turned legs and arm supports and the feeble carved cresting that accentuates the triple-humped shape of the back still assert the influence of carver and frame-maker, but it is a diminished influence.

SECTION 16. REGENCY TO EARLY VICTORIAN

The Greek revival, generated in the 1760s, was the chief formative influence in the design of furniture during the first quarter of the 19th century, and the elegance of the neo-Greek style owed much to the work of Thomas Hope (1770–1831), but far more to a fresh conception of curvilinear design that followed the reappearance of shapes that were originated and perfected by Greek craftsmen in the 6th and 5th centuries B.C. The change from the graceful but rather staid lines of late 18th century furniture was particularly marked in chairs, and although designers like Thomas Sheraton gave the name Grecian to some examples of seat furniture depicted in their works, they justified the description by using Greek ornament, and were not influenced by the reappearance of the *klismos*, that ancient Greek chair which allowed people to sit in a relaxed, comfortable position without loss of dignity. The *klismos* had concave legs that splayed outwards, the back legs and uprights forming a continuous curve, with the uprights crossed at the top by a shallow, concave back rest, rectangular in shape. In Thomas Hope's versions of the *klismos* the continuity of the long back curve was broken at seat level, and sometimes he added arms to the design, as shown on page 212. The original Greek chair had been single, for arms appeared only on ceremonial thrones or privileged seats. The shallow concave back rest of the *klismos* was repeated by the rectangular tablet that formed the top rail of many early 19th century chairs and projected slightly beyond the back uprights; a type that was given the contemporary name of "tablet top".

The style that developed after this new curvilinear revolution in design flourished until the late 1820s, and many of its characteristic features, especially in chairs, survived until the early Victorian period. George, Prince of Wales, was Prince Regent from 1811 until 1820, when his father died and he became George IV; but although the Regency lasted only nine years it has since been associated by name with the gracious maturity of the Greek revival. It had some features in common with the French Empire style, for designers in both countries used the same antique sources for ornamental prototypes, but the character of Regency furniture was wholly different from the spirited imperialism of contemporary French design. The term "English Empire,"

Drawing room, designed by Thomas Hope, with paintings of oriental scenes on the walls. The deep armchairs decorated with a chimera on the side panels, the long fixed seats with lion-headed sphinxes at each end, the table supported by monopodia, a sphinx head above a lion's leg, and the stools with their X-shaped under frames, are examples of drawing-board design. No practical chairmaker could have conceived the graceless shapes of those armchairs in the opening decade of the 19th century. Like the interior on the opposite page and the chairs below, this is reproduced on a smaller scale from Hope's book, *Household Furniture and Interior Decoration* (1807).

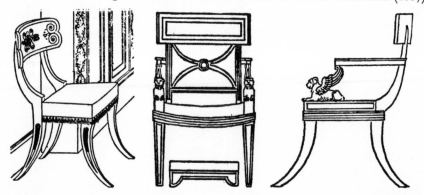

The influence of the Greek *klismos* on chairs designed by Hope. Variations of the tablet-top persisted until the middle of the century. In the Greek original, back legs and uprights formed a graceful, continuous line: Hope broke the line at seat level.

probably coined by some dealer or collector in the early years of the present century, is not only misleading but meaningless. A long war had severed communications between France and England, and when relations were resumed in 1802, the peace was short-lived. A purely superficial resemblance between French Empire and Regency furniture was extended when interest in Egyptian ornament was stimulated by Denon's *Voyages dans la Basse et Haute Egypt*, published in 1802, which became available in England during the brief peace. Thomas Hope flirted with an Egyptian style, how ineffectively may be judged from the illustration below; sphinxs' heads appeared on the ends of chair arms, or emerged from terms, like those on the commode and chimney glass on page 215, or took the form of monopodia, like those supporting the table in Hope's design for a drawing room on page 212.

Continued on page 221

Interior by Hope, designed in what was described as the Egyptian style. The armchairs and the seat show the influence of the Greek Revival, but like the furniture in the drawing room opposite, they are typical productions by a professional "man of taste".

213

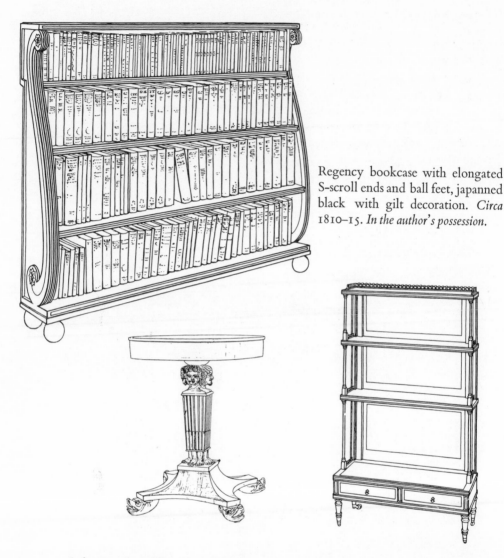

Regency bookcase with elongated S-scroll ends and ball feet, japanned black with gilt decoration. *Circa 1810–15. In the author's possession.*

Left: Circular table of satinwood, partly polished, partly ebonised; the heads and feet of the quadruple herm that forms the supporting pillar as well as the lower third of the moulded sheath are gilded. The base is supported on dog's heads; the top is of black marble. *Circa* 1810–15. *Formerly in the collection of the late Robert Atkinson, F.R.I.B.A. Right*: Open bookcase in satinwood, with two drawers in the base and a gilded brass gallery on the upper shelf. *Circa* 1800–10. *In the possession of Mrs V. Atkins.*

Chimney glass, with three panels, in mahogany frame, carved and gilt. *Circa* 1810. The frieze is flanked by terms with sphinx's heads, with slightly tapering fluted sheaths below, from which human feet project to form a base. (Compare this device with the shaft and base of the table opposite and the commode below.) *Formerly in the possession of the late Mrs Frances Evans.*

Bow-fronted commode in softwood, with pen and ink decoration on a black ground, flanked by Egyptian terms, carved and gilt. This Egyptian motif appears on the chimney glass above. The commode is supported on turned feet. There is a frieze drawer below the top, and the cupboard doors have a gilt wire grille backed by pleated silk. *Circa* 1810–20. *In the Victoria and Albert Museum.*

Left: Satinwood table with drop leaves which form an oval top when extended. Inlaid with thin lines of boxwood. *Circa* 1800. *In the possession of Mrs V. Atkins. Right:* Circular-topped library table with drawers in the frieze. The fluted supporting pillar rises from a base with three concave sides; the carved paw feet are surmounted by winged volutes. Mahogany gilt. *Circa* 1805–10. A comparable example is in the Royal Pavilion, Brighton.

Above: Library table in dark mahogany cross-banded with inlaid lines of boxwood, *Circa* 1800. Similar to an example in the Royal Pavilion, Brighton. The extremely simple lines of this table give the fullest decorative value to the finely figured mahogany veneers on the top and drawer fronts.

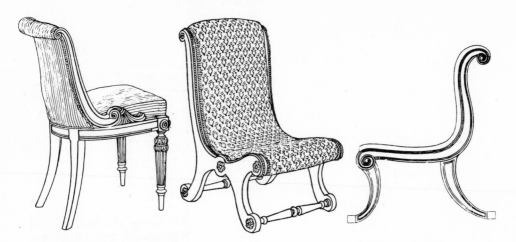

Left: Gilt chair with back formed by elongated S-scroll, turned and reeded front legs and swept back legs. *Circa* 1810. From an example in the King's bedroom of the Royal Pavilion, Brighton. *Centre:* A low-seated Regency armless chair, japanned black with twisted brass wire gilt inlaid on seat and back rails, and brass patrae at the scroll ends and centre of seat rail. *In the author's possession. Right:* Scroll-backed chair with sabre legs, that, like the chairs on page 212, is derived from the Greek *klismos.* Reproduced on a slightly smaller scale from Thomas Hope's *Household Furniture and Interior Decoration* (1807).

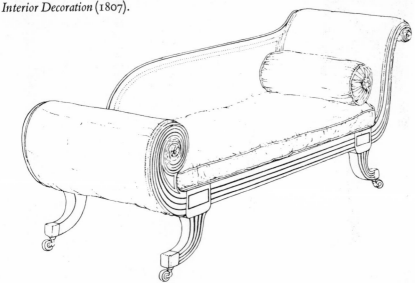

Scroll-ended sofa in black, decorated with thin incised gilt lines. *Circa* 1805. In the collection at the Royal Pavilion, Brighton, South drawing room. All the examples of seat furniture on this page show the influence of the new curvilinear revolution in design that was concurrent with the Greek revival.

Right: The term "arc-back" for this type of Greek revival chair is not contemporary, and the design lacks the easy grace of the *klismos*. Compare this with the chairs on page 212. *Circa* 1800–05.

Two single chairs, with modified tablet tops, and the characteristic elegance of the Regency style. Both are in mahogany. *Left: Formerly in the possession of the late Mrs Frances Evans. Right: In the Author's possession.* (See examples on page 212.) *Circa* 1810–15.

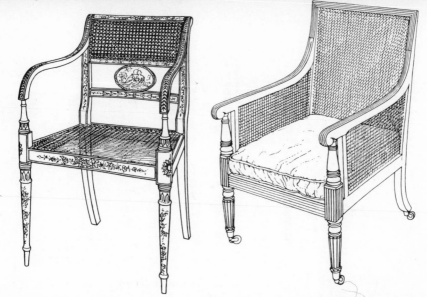

Left: Elbow chair with frame japanned black and decorated with floral motifs. The oval panel that unites the middle rail with the caned panel is painted with a classical subject. *Circa* 1800. *In the possession of Mrs V. Atkins. Right:* Mahogany *bergère* with caned back, sides and seat. *Circa* 1805. *In the possession of Julian Gloag.*

Two armchairs designed by Thomas Sheraton and reproduced from Plate 3 of *The Cabinet Dictionary* (1803).

219

Left: Armchair with dipped wooden seat. A country-made version in oak of contemporary Regency fashions. *Centre:* A lattice-back elbow chair in mahogany. *Circa* 1800. (There is a comparable example in Sir John Soane's Museum.) *Right:* Armchair in softwood, carved in low relief, with paw feet and lion-headed terminals to the arms: painted and gilt. From a design by George Smith, included in *A Collection of Designs for Household Furniture and Interior Decoration, in the Most Approved and Elegant Taste,* a work first issued in two parts in 1805 and subsequently incorporated in a book of 158 plates that was published in 1808. Designs like this suggest that "Elegant Taste" was beginning to decline. *Victoria and Albert Museum.*

Left and centre: Two drawing room chairs reproduced on a smaller scale from plate 34 of *The Modern Style of Cabinet Work,* published by T. King (second edition, 1832). *Right:* Elbow chair in mahogany. *Circa* 1830–35. *In the author's possession.* All three examples show lingering traces of the Greek Revival, but with the exception of the chair on the left they have lost the elegance of the Regency style.

One of the characteristics of the decoration of Regency furniture was a subtle and restrained use of ormolu mounts and inlaid lines of brass or silver. Sheraton described this tendency when he wrote, in *The Cabinet Dictionary*, that "brass beads, and small lines of brass, are now much in use in the English furniture, and looks very handsome in black rose and other dark woods." Thin bands of ornamental patterns, such as the Greek key, were inlaid in brass on ebony; shining metallic lines accentuated curves and scrolls, and on japanned furniture, such as the scroll-ended bookcase on page 214, fluting and hollow mouldings were gilded.

Sheratons's last work was *The Cabinet-Maker, Upholsterer, and General Artists' Encyclopaedia,* of which one volume only was published in 1805, the year of his death; many of the plates disclose a diminished regard for elegance, symptomatic of coming changes in taste, also forecast by the over-emphatic boldness of line occasionally apparent in the designs of George Smith, who published a series of plates in two parts, fifty in each, between December 1804 and July 1805. These were subsequently included in a volume containing 158 plates, issued in 1808 and entitled *A Collection of Designs for Household Furniture and Interior Decoration.* Smith's plates record many variations of the Regency

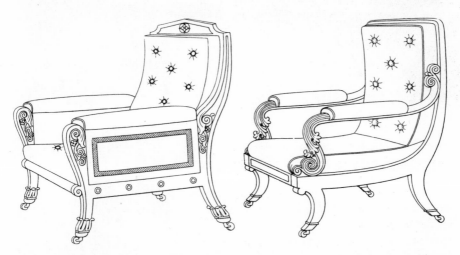

Two easy chairs reproduced on a smaller scale from plates 29 and 36 of *The Modern Style of Cabinet Work*, published by T. King (second edition, 1832). Elegance has been unable to compete with comfort: these designs are merely decorative frames for deep cushions and buttoned upholstery. The classic ornament used is coarsely executed and ill-placed.

Above: Interior of the saloon, Eaton Hall, Cheshire, built between 1804 and 1812. Late Georgian Gothic, with furniture in the contemporary Regency style. Reproduced on a smaller scale from *Views of Eaton Hall*, by J. C. Buckler (1826). *Right:* So-called "Monastic" chair, made up from fragments of Gothic woodwork. Reproduced from *A Walk from London to Fulham*, by Crofton Croker (London: William Tegg, 1860).

222

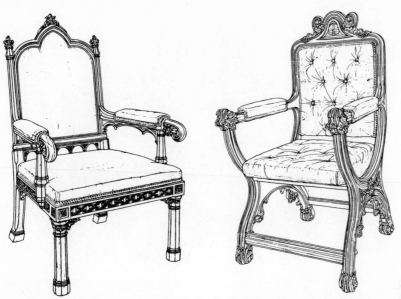

Left: Armchair of carved and gilded beechwood, designed in the Gothic taste, but conceived in the classic tradition, like the Eaton Hall interior opposite and other examples of what may be called "Gentlemen's Gothic." *Circa* 1825. *Right:* Armchair of carved oak, designed by A. W. N. Pugin, the dedicated Gothic revivalist who almost alone of his contemporaries was capable of recreating the spirit of mediaeval art. Made for the dining-room at Scarisbrick Hall, Lancashire, about 1837. *Both chairs in the Victoria and Albert Museum.*

style, and include designs for Gothic furniture, which differed from the "Monastic" Gothic of the so-called "Abbotsford" period. That term, invented in the late 19th century, was derived from the house built in Roxburghshire for Sir Walter Scott. "Monastic" furniture was either made up from fragments of mediaeval woodwork, church stalls and pew ends, like the chair opposite, or else designed in the belief, as Pugin said when condemning the methods of upholsterers, "that nothing can be Gothic unless it is found in some church. Hence your modern man," he continued, "designs a sofa or an occasional table from details culled out of Britton's Cathedrals. . . ." Such casually borrowed ornament was often badly copied and meanly executed; only an artist of genius like Pugin could impart to the furniture he designed the vehement vitality of mediaeval work. The late Georgian Gothic chair above is, by comparison with Pugin's design that appears beside it, as remote from the spirit of Gothic tradition as the "Monastic" example on page 222.

The light, gay Georgian graces were gradually obliterated, and were on the way out when John Claudius Loudon's *Encyclopaedia of Cottage, Farm, and*

Continued on page 230

Above: An attempt to revive a "Norman" style was made by the architect, Edward Buckton Lamb (1805–69), who designed this furnished interior which was published in *The Architectural Magazine,* Vol. I, 1834, November, page 338. Apart from the octagonal table with its central pillar and four columnar legs, the chairs, which Lamb said were inspired by the seated figures of kings, queens and bishops in a set of "ancient chessmen of Norman character" in the British Museum, are typical of the so-called "Abbotsford" period. (See "Monastic" chair on page 222.)

Gothic chair with heraldic devices, designed by E. B. Lamb and reproduced from J.C. Loudon's *Encyclopaedia of Cottage, Farm and Villa Architecture and Furniture,* first published in 1833. While such designs, which claimed an old English ancestry, were multiplied on the drawing boards of the ignorant, a long and vivacious tradition of chair-making in country districts had perfected the Windsor

type, like the example at the right, with its double bow back, spur stretcher and cabriole front legs. (See low-back type on page 195.)

224

Library bookcase in mahogany with a broken front, attached Doric columns at the angles of the lower part, and arched glazed doors. *Circa* 1835–45. The design marks the transition from late Georgian to the Victorian vernacular style. *In the possession of Bayliss, Jones & Bayliss Ltd., Wolverhampton.*

Right: Mahogany davenport, *circa* 1820. A compact type of writing-desk invented in the late 18th century, and made originally by the firm of Gillow for a Captain Davenport. *In the Victoria and Albert Museum.* During the second quarter of the century, the form of the davenport changed. Both examples shown below are in walnut. The elaborate type on the left has carved cabriole supports for the desk, and a rising bank of drawers and pigeon holes at the back. *Circa* 1845–50. (*In the possession of Stanley Pollitt, Esq.*) That on the right has columns supporting the desk, and the four drawers at the side are enclosed by a door. *Circa* 1835–45. *In the possession of Mrs Alan Deller.*

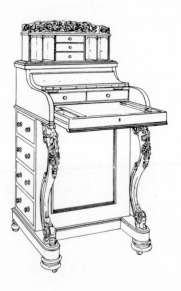

Mahogany sideboard with spiral turning on the front legs and inlaid lines of boxwood. *Circa* 1815–30.

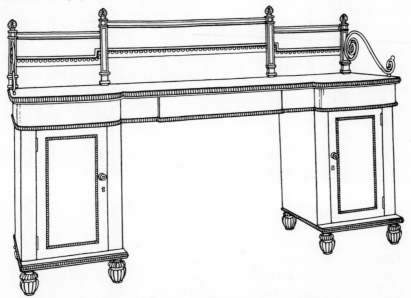

Pedestal sideboard in mahogany, with gilt brass rails surrounding the top and drawers
below. Gadrooning ornaments the mouldings above and below the frieze and also
appears on the inset panels and the bases of the pedestals. *Circa* 1825–35.

Sideboard and sarcophagus, designed by Richard Bridgens and included in *Furniture with Candelabra and Interior Decoration*. (London: William Pickering, 1838.) The restraint of Georgian Gothic survived throughout the second quarter of the century.

Left: Bookcase in the Gothic taste, reproduced on a smaller scale from plate 68 of *The Modern Style of Cabinet Work*, published by T. King. (London: second edition, 1832.) *Right:* Mahogany chiffonier, equipped as a sideboard with drawers and shelves behind the doors. The back is bordered by C-scrolls and rather coarsely carved acanthus foliations. An early example of the Victorian vernacular style. *Circa 1845–50. In the possession of Mrs G. M. Gloag.*

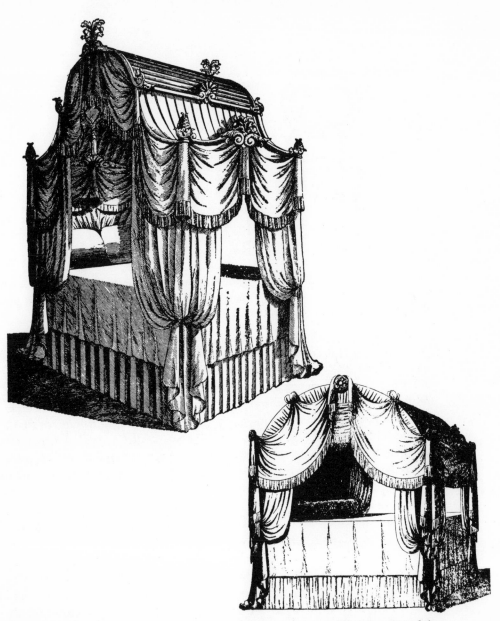

Until the introduction of the metal bedstead, beds during the first decades of the
19th century tended to be overwhelmed by draperies: upholsterers produced
sculptural effects with fabrics, almost as ambitious and extravagantly fanciful as the
state beds of the late 17th century. Both these designs, the tent bed *right*, and the
field bed *left*, are dated 1827, and are reproduced on a slightly smaller scale from
the 1836 edition of George Smith's *The Cabinet Makers' and Upholsterers' Guide*.

229

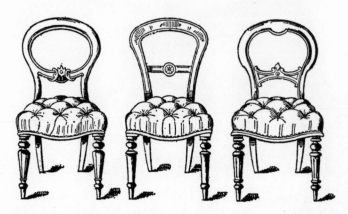

Balloon-back dining-room chairs with buttoned upholstery, reproduced from a trade catalogue by an unknown maker, *circa* 1840–50. The most familiar and characteristic examples of the Victorian vernacular style.

Villa Architecture, and Furniture was first published in 1833. Loudon reproduced many of the illustrations of furniture in his *Encyclopaedia* from the portfolios and warehouses of the principal London manufacturers, and those rather indifferent drawings show the crude, opening phase of the Early Victorian style, that developed in the 1840s, and retained some of the attributes of classic design. The library bookcase on page 225 marks the transition from late Georgian to Victorian. In the decade before the Great Exhibition of 1851, the last authentic furniture style emerged. This has been described as Victorian vernacular. As a style it was distinctive, with its air of solidity and frank concessions to comfort, satisfying proportions, relative freedom from excessive ornament, and such characteristic forms as the balloon-back chair. It was happily adjusted to the needs of prosperous and respectable householders with its polished mahogany and bouncing, buttoned leather upholstery. But the reckless confusion of taste that followed the Great Exhibition replaced it with such a plethora of historic and exotic styles—Gothic, Byzantine, Indian, and even a limp revival of rococo—that by the 1860s it was deemed hopelessly old-fashioned. With it ended a tradition of good design that had endured for four centuries.

INDEX

Names and places are included. When the reference is to a caption, the page number is shown in italics, thus: *98*.

231